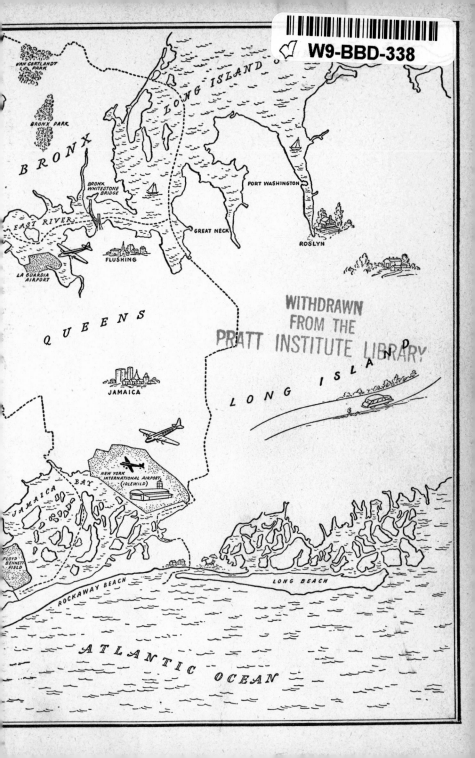

VAN CORTLANDT PARK

LONG ISLAND SOUND

BRONX PARK

BRONX

BRONX WHITESTONE BRIDGE

EAST RIVER

PORT WASHINGTON

GREAT NECK

ROSLYN

FLUSHING

LA GUARDIA AIRPORT

QUEENS

JAMAICA

LONG ISLAND

NEW YORK INTERNATIONAL AIRPORT (IDLEWILD)

JAMAICA BAY

FLOYD BENNETT FIELD

ROCKAWAY BEACH

LONG BEACH

ATLANTIC OCEAN

NEW YORK CITY
OLD AND NEW

WALL STREET IN 1830

Wall Street is today the most important business street in the world. A hundred years ago it was lined with pleasant homes.

(From an old print in the New York Historical Society)

NEW YORK CITY
OLD AND NEW

by

Caroline D. Emerson

*Illustrated by Alida Conover and
James MacDonald*

NEW AND FULLY REVISED EDITION OF
"OLD NEW YORK FOR YOUNG NEW YORKERS"

NEW YORK　　E. P. DUTTON & CO., INC.　PUBLISHERS

LIBRARY OF CONGRESS CATALOG CARD NUMBER: 53-6071

AMERICAN BOOK—STRATFORD PRESS, INC., NEW YORK

TO
A.M.S.

CONTENTS

Chapter One

THE NIGHT PLANE

THE sea gulls screamed and flapped their great gray wings. Then they rose in a whirling cloud above the water of the East River. The night plane for Washington roared through the air. The sea gulls circled below it, but they kept well out of its way.

Over New York City roared the plane. The five boroughs of the city lay like a map below it. The plane had taken off from Idlewild in the Borough of Queens. Now it flew past Brooklyn toward Manhattan. Far below it were the bridges over the East River. Steamers and barges and tugboats looked like toys.

High above the United Nations Building flew the plane, past the sharp point of the Chrysler Building and the proud tower of the Empire State. To the south lay the harbor and the Borough of Richmond on Staten Island. Far to the north lay the Bronx.

The sun was setting over the Hudson River. Into a flaming sunset cloud flew the plane. Its red and green lights flashed on and off. The sea gulls could see little use in red and green lights. They knew enough not to run into each other. Back on the East River they settled down for the night.

Tall buildings were lighting up. Forty, fifty, sixty stories high rose the lights. The bridges were streamers of lights. Tiny lighted cars and busses hurried across them. Tugboats all lighted up like birthday cakes scurried under them. Everyone was hurrying home from work. The gulls settled down peacefully on the rocks. The city might hurry and roar about them. But the gulls slept in peace.

So their fathers had slept before them, and their fathers' fathers—and so on back for hundreds and thousands of years. But those earlier gulls had looked upon far different sights.

The rocks were the same. The East River was the same, but instead of tall buildings all aglow with light, deep woods covered the land. Instead of ferryboats and ocean liners cutting through the blue water of the harbor, Indian canoes glided by. Instead of busses and trucks grinding over hard paved streets, Indian boys ran swiftly down forest paths. Instead of planes roaring over head, the sea gulls had the air pretty much to themselves.

Instead of people, people, people everywhere, deer, bears, and wolves roamed through the forest. Rabbits hopped through the tangles of wild grapevines. Porcupines rattled their quills. Beavers worked in the swamps.

In winter, heavy snow fell on the great oak trees. It covered the roofs of the Indian lodges in the tiny villages. In the stillness of a winter's night, a panther would cry out. Indian babies would creep closer to their mothers. The men and boys would throw wood on the fires.

In summer, Indian boys hunted and fished. Indian girls picked wild grapes and ate wild strawberries. The trees were filled with birds singing most sweetly.

"They are the spirits of our friends who have left us," said the Indian women.

Only a few sea gulls stayed in summer. Summer was a busy time for them. They flew North for nesting on the coast of Maine or Labrador. Only a few young birds stayed behind, and those of the older birds who had decided not to raise families that year.

Chapter Two

FOUR HUNDRED YEARS AGO

ON THE shores of the East River sat Indian women
working. The sea gulls swooped above their heads
and screamed to each other. The women were opening
oysters and stringing them on twigs to dry in the sun.
The gulls flew about trying to catch tidbits.

"Thieves!" cried the women as they threw stones at
the gulls. "Go fish for yourselves!"

But you can't teach a sea gull what belongs to him and
what belongs to someone else, and it's no good trying.

Out on the river two boys were fishing with bits of
sharp pointed bone for fishhooks. The boys floated in a
dugout canoe. The canoe was cleverly made from the
trunk of a great tulip tree. The boys had helped their
father make it.

First they had made a fire by rubbing together two dry
sticks. Then, little by little, they had burned away the
inside of a big log that they had chosen. Carefully they
had scraped away the charred wood with sharp stones.
It had been slow work. The gulls wondered at the trouble
men took. They did not need boats.

Now and again the boys threw away a small fish. The

INDIAN MAKING A DUGOUT CANOE
(Detail from an old print by De Brie)

gulls fought over the fish while the boys watched, laughing.

On shore a little papoose woke up and cried. He was bound to a wooden board for a cradle. His mother gave him a turkey bone to suck. Then she picked him up and hung him on her back. She called to the boys in the canoe. One of them stood up in the bow of the boat. He was straight and tall. His body was a reddish brown. His heavy black hair fell to his shoulders. Gracefully he dived into the water. With swift strong strokes he swam ashore. He waited to help the other boy drag the heavy canoe from the water and hide it safely in the bushes. Then he jumped from rock to rock until he reached his mother.

"Look," he cried as he pointed to the sun. It looked strangely round and red as it sank into a sunset cloud.

"Our Elder-Brother-The-Sun is weary from his long

journey across the sky," said his mother. "He goes to his home in the West. We, too, must go home."

The women picked up their baskets. They walked down a narrow trail through the woods to the village. It was dark in the woods, but it was lighter as they came out into the cornfield that surrounded the houses. The cornstalks grew several feet apart. Bean vines grew up the stalks. Big pumpkins were ripening on the ground between. Corn, beans, and pumpkins, "the three sisters that give us life," the Indians called them.

Carefully the women had planted the seeds in the spring "when the birch tree leaf was the size of a mouse's ear." They had tended the young plants with hoes made of the shoulder bone of wolf or deer. Now the corn was nearly ripe. Some ears would be roasted by the fire and eaten. Most of the ears would be dried and pounded into corn meal. Many would be buried for winter use.

The two boys dodged among the cornstalks. How close to the village could they creep without arousing the village dogs? Suddenly the quiet of the evening was broken by the fierce howls of dogs. The boys jumped to their feet with a war whoop, and raced each other to the lodge in which they lived.

Some of the houses in the village were round. Others were as much as a hundred feet long. They were made of tough young trees driven into the ground. The tops were bent over in an arch. Sheets of bark and mats of rushes covered the frame. Holes in the roof let out the smoke from the fires below.

Several families lived in each long house. Each family had its own fire, its wooden bowls and clay jars, its pile of bearskins for beds. From the roof of the house hung

INDIAN LODGES

The large hut was for several families, the smaller was for one. The smaller one is not finished and you can see the framework under the bark mats. Beside it is a rack of green twigs to hold fish over the fire and a mortar for grinding corn into meal. The mortar is made from the trunk of a tree.

strings of dried corn, dried meat and fish for winter eating.

The boys poked among the ashes. They pulled out charred cornhusks. Inside each was a warm corncake that their mother had left baking. It was made of corn meal mixed with water and sweetened with maple sugar.

Then the boys threw more wood on the ashes and toasted strips of venison. The juice sizzled on the red coals. The dogs smelled it. Yap-yap-yap they howled, but they did not dare come in the door. The boys munched their meat. It was half raw and half burned.

Their mother joined them. She unlaced the thongs of the baby board. The baby lay on a wolf skin while the boys played with him. He waved his arms and kicked his legs. They must grow straight and strong if he were to grow to be a great hunter.

Suddenly there came from outside the boom-boom-boom of a drum. The boys' father stooped as he came through the low door of the lodge. He was six feet tall. His hair stood up in a ruff on top of his head. The hair at the sides had been burned away with hot stones, and only one long lock hung at his back. He was dressed in a beautiful ceremonial suit of deerskin decorated with dyed porcupine quills. A cloak of tiny feathers hung from his shoulder. Each feather was fastened in the net of hemp string that held the cloak together. His face was painted red, yellow, and black. His body was tattooed.

There was to be a dance the next day for the great autumn hunt was soon to take place. The boys must practice with him their parts in the dance and song. Boom-boom-boom went the drums.

Hunters were gathering from far and near. They would spread out through the woods and drive the deer, the bears, and panthers toward one of the rivers. Other hunters would be waiting there with their six-foot bows and swift arrows. But first the hunters would dance to call on the spirits of the animals to give them food that their people might live. The Indians did not kill for pleasure. They killed only what they needed.

Boom-boom-boom went the drums. The boys followed their father in the steps of the dance. They raised their hands high above their heads.

"Ho-oo!" they shouted. Twelve times they shouted that the great Manitou in the highest heaven might hear. The medicine man came into the lodge. He wore a great carved wooden mask and a bearskin. He sat by the fire and repeated with the boys the words of the chant.

Boom-boom-boom went the drums. On went the songs and dances late into the night. At last the boys threw themselves down upon their bearskins. The fires burned low. It was dark and quiet in the village. On the rocks in the East River the sea gulls were sleeping peacefully.

So Algonquin Indians lived where New York stands today. The forest gave them wood for their houses. The women sewed the deerskin and furs for their clothes. Fish from the water, deer from the forest, corn from their little fields gave them food. Wood fires gave them heat and light. They did not need coal dug from the earth or oil to be brought every day in barges and tankers. They did not need great electrical plants to turn the coal into electricity. There was wood on Manhattan for their light and heat. But out on the rocks on the East River the sea gulls kept themselves warm. When the sun went down, they went to sleep. They saw no reason for sitting up after dark.

Sometimes today when men are digging in the ground to lay the foundation for a tall building, they find clay jars that once Indian women used. They find stone knives that some Indian boys once dropped as they ran down forest paths. Once they found a dugout canoe by the water's edge. They find blackened campfires.

They find many, many piles of shells. Some shells have been ground away to make the precious shell beads called wampum. White wampum came from the periwinkle shells. Purple wampum was made from the hard clam shell. Wampum was money and gold and jewels to the Indians.

The sea gulls never could understand about wampum any more than they can understand about money today.

"You can't eat it?" say the young sea gulls. "It doesn't keep you warm? Why do men want it?"

But the old sea gulls only shake their heads, and tell the young sea gulls not to ask so many questions.

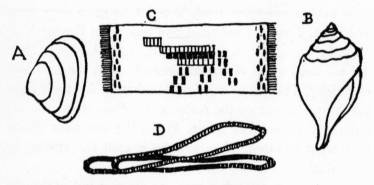

A. CLAM SHELL   C. WAMPUM BELT
B. PERIWINKLE SHELL   D. STRING OF WAMPUM

"THE HALF MOON"

The sails were square. The stern was high. There was a red lion under the bowsprit.

Chapter Three

STRANGE HAPPENINGS IN 1609

A LITTLE kittiwake gull brought the news. The kittiwakes live far out at sea, and only come near shore once in a while.

"There's a gull out there as big as an island," screamed the kittiwake. "It has wings that it keeps spread even when it's floating on the water. It's coming this way."

Once or twice before great birds had sailed by. These monsters carried men on their backs. In 1524 an Italian named Verrazzano had sailed past. But Verrazzano did not stay. He did not seem to care for the land of the Manhattan Indians. For Verrazzano was searching for a strait to take him to the Pacific Ocean.

Men who talked English had passed by. A Negro explorer from Portugal, Estavan Gomez, had sailed near. But this newcomer did not float away. It came very close to land. Then it folded its wings and floated quietly upon the water.

Indians hurried down to the shore. Swift runners were sent to gather warriors together.

Some Indians said, "It is a great monster."

Some said, "It is a huge fish."

Then runners brought back word: "There are men upon it. They are not like us. They have pale faces."

"There is one," was the next word, "who wears a red cloak. He must be the great Manitou."

But the gulls had just made a discovery of their own. "That thing isn't a gull at all," they cried. "It's a monstrous canoe."

The gulls flew all about the ship. She was about the size of a tugboat of today and she had three masts. She was very gay. Her bow was painted green with red and yellow ornaments. Under her bowsprit was a red lion. Her stern was painted blue with white clouds and yellow stars and a moon. The *Half Moon* was her name.

The *Half Moon* flew a Dutch flag with orange, white, and blue stripes across it. She had come from the city of Amsterdam in Holland. Half of her twenty sailors were Dutch. Half were English. Her captain was a "skillful English pilot" named Henry Hudson.

Now Henry Hudson like Verrazzano and Gomez was not interested in this new world that Columbus had discovered. He cared nothing for a huge new country full of Indians and forests and wild beasts. He wanted to find a way to get through America so that ships could sail directly from Europe to Asia. He wished to buy a cargo of silks and velvets, or spices such as cinnamon and pepper, nutmeg and allspice, or sugar and candied fruits, ivories and rare jewels to carry back to Europe.

For more than a hundred years men had been trying to find this passageway to India and China. Some men had sailed to the South, but it was a long dangerous voyage around South America. Some had sailed to the North but they had found icebergs and frozen seas.

"Let me try," begged Henry Hudson.

Some merchants in Amsterdam gave him a ship to command. Away to the North he sailed, but he found only the icy Arctic Ocean. He turned his ship around, but he did not sail back to Holland. For Hudson had a letter and rough map from a friend, Captain John Smith.

People did not know much about this strange new land of America as yet, but, little by little, explorers were finding out more. This new map showed a place where water stretched far inland. Where did that water go? That was the question. No white man knew the answer.

"Perhaps," thought Hudson as he studied the map, "perhaps that waterway is a strait that leads right through America. Perhaps one can sail through it to the Pacific Ocean. Perhaps this is the short way to Asia."

But perhaps it was only a river that grew smaller and smaller until it was only a brook. Hudson decided to sail down the coast of America to that waterway, and to find out whether it was a river or a strait. He did not have permission from the owners of the *Half Moon,* but he went anyway. If he were successful they would forget that.

And so on the second day of September in 1609, Hudson anchored the *Half Moon* in the outer bay which leads to what we call today New York Harbor. All was quiet except for the cries of the sea gulls as they flew around the ship.

Hudson ordered his men to lower a small boat. He sent several sailors ashore to see what the land was like. Later one of them wrote, "The lands were as pleasant with grass and flowers and goodly trees as any they had ever seen and very sweet smells came therefrom."

But something was soon to happen that was not so pleasant. From shore came two canoes, filled with Indians. The red men wanted to find out more about these newcomers. Were they friend or foe? The Indians were fearful. One raised his bow and arrow and shot. An English sailor named John Coleman dropped dead in the bottom of the boat. The white men did not fire back for it had begun to rain. Lighted fuses were needed to fire the guns in those days. The rain had put out the fuses. The guns would not go off. The canoes paddled quickly away.

Night came on. There was wind and rain. The little boat could not find its way back to the *Half Moon.* All night it floated about in the darkness. Morning came at last. Back to the big ship went the little boat. The men were wet and miserable. Later they rowed sadly ashore and buried their comrade, Coleman.

The sea gulls cried out against what the red men had done, but later they were to find out that the white man could do just as unpleasant things as the Indians.

The sea gulls had much to learn.

Chapter Four

A RIVER OR A STRAIT

THE next day, Hudson sailed the *Half Moon* through the Narrows into the upper bay. Manhattan Island lay before him. The land was marshy near the shore, but the center of the island was hilly. Heavy forests covered it, with here and there an opening that showed where the Indians planted their corn and tobacco. Streams and brooks ran down the hillsides. It was a pleasant land.

To the west of Manhattan lay the broad waterway that Hudson had sailed for eight weeks across the Atlantic to explore. Where did this waterway lead? Was it only a

27

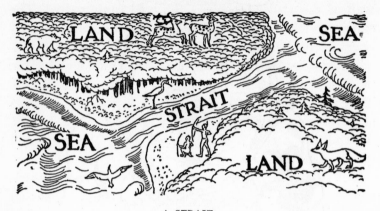

A STRAIT

A strait is a waterway through which ships can sail to more water beyond.

river that led far back inland? Did it grow smaller and smaller until it was only a brook that a boy could jump across? Or was it by chance a wide strait that led through to the Pacific Ocean? That was the great question.

That day many Indians paddled out to the *Half Moon*. The white men traded axes, knives, mirrors, and red cloth for beaver furs. The Dutch were delighted to get beaver fur so cheap. The furs would sell for much money in Amsterdam. The red men marveled at the sharpness of the white men's tools. Both sides were pleased with the day's trading. Everything went smoothly at first.

Then Hudson decided to hold two young Indians as prisoners. He wanted to take them back to Holland to show what the wild men from this new land were like. Other explorers had brought back prisoners. Hudson ordered his men to lock two Indians in a small cabin. Away up the waterway sailed the *Half Moon*.

She sailed past the north end of the island where rocky cliffs came down to the water's edge. She sailed past the wall of the Palisades where the bald eagle nested. The sailors watched eagerly to see what lay ahead. The prisoners in the stuffy cabin below were forgotten.

But as the *Half Moon* rode at anchor that night, the prisoners crawled through a porthole and swam ashore. They were glad to be free. It was good to feel their bodies slide through the clear, cold water. But in their hearts, the Indians carried fear and hate for the white man and his ways. One can hardly blame them.

For twenty days the *Half Moon* sailed up the mysterious waterway. She passed vast woodlands. She passed mountains that came down to the very shore. She passed Indian villages. But no great ocean opened up ahead. Each day the banks came closer. The water grew shallower. Then it no longer tasted salt. At last it was clear that this was a river and not a strait.

When the *Half Moon* could go no farther, Hudson sent a small boat for twenty-seven miles more just to be sure that the Pacific Ocean did not lie ahead. But it did no good. Then Hudson ordered the sailors to turn the *Half Moon* about. He knew for certain that this was a river, and he named it the Great River of the Mountains, and so it was called until the English named it for Hudson himself. Down the Great River sailed the *Half Moon*.

The white men traded with the Indians along the way. The chiefs of the tribes gave feasts for them. They broke their arrows and threw them in the fire to show that they were friendly. But farther down the river things did not go as well.

One day an Indian paddled out to the *Half Moon*. He was curious about these mysterious strangers and their possessions. He reached through an open porthole and helped himself to two shirts, a pillow, and a belt. Never had he seen such strange things before! He handled them in amazement. Then the ship's mate discovered him. He hit the Indian with a sword and killed him.

Other sailors lowered a boat to try to save their possessions. Angry Indians, who were watching from shore, swam out and tried to upset the boat. The ship's cook struck at another Indian and killed him. So that made two men lost, and hard feelings on both sides.

Then something happened that surprised the Indians and amazed the sea gulls. The white men set fire to a black log that stood on the deck of the ship. The strange log roared like thunder. It flashed forth lightning. It hurled stones across the water that killed Indians even on shore.

A canoe filled with Indians was broken to pieces by one. The men struggled in the water. The wounded were drowned. The sea gulls did not wait for more. They screamed and flew away as fast as they could go.

Then down to the lower bay sailed the *Half Moon,* through the Narrows and off to the open sea. Home to Holland she went.

The sea gulls hoped it was the last of her! They did not want men coming back to these parts and making so much noise.

Some of the Indians felt the same way, but others thought of the wonderful tools and weapons that the white men had. They longed for a chance to trade for more of them. For the Indians had no iron or steel. They had a little copper, but they did not know how to make sharp-edged knives and tools. They had no gunpowder. Steel and gunpowder were what made the white man so powerful. Steel and gunpowder were what the Indians wanted.

Henry Hudson never came back to Manhattan Island, but other men came for Hudson and his sailors told of the rich furs that could be had so cheaply from the Indians. They told of the great forests of oaks and chestnuts, tulip trees and hickory where timber could be cut.

Hudson himself still longed to find the passageway to Asia. Once again he started off. This time he sailed again to the North to try to get around North America. The sea became full of icebergs. The days were cold and dreary. The sailors feared shipwreck and death. They turned against Hudson. They refused to go farther.

Hudson ordered them to sail on, but they mutinied and rose up against him. At last they put Hudson, his young son, and seven sick sailors in a small boat. They set the boat adrift in the cold, black sea. There they left them, while the big ship sailed for home. What happened to Hudson and his young son and the seven sailors none but the sea gulls know.

Chapter Five

THE FUR TRADERS

THE white men did come back to Manhattan Island, all too soon to please the sea gulls. Several times a year a ship would come sailing quietly into the harbor. The sea gulls would wait until they were sure no cannon were to be fired. Then they flew about the ship trying to pick up news and stray bits of food.

Small boats rowed back and forth from the big ship to trade with the Indians. Beaver, mink, marten, bear, and fox skins were exchanged for blankets, knives, kettles, awls, and beads. When the trading was over, the ships would set sail and glide out of the harbor. The sea gulls would fly as far as they felt like going. Then they would turn back to the quiet of the East River.

After a few years the white men needed a place on land

to store their furs. About 1614 they built a few rough huts. Up the Great River near where Albany stands to-day, they built a log fort on an island in the river. They called all the country along the Great River, New Nether-land, for Holland was part of the Netherlands and these traders came from Holland.

One of the men was named Adrian Block. His ship was called *The Tiger*. One cold November day when Block and his men were near Manhattan Island, a terrible thing happened. *The Tiger* caught on fire. The men had to plunge overboard to save their lives. They swam ashore through the icy water, but they were helpless to save their ship. *The Tiger* burned to the water line and then sank.

The sea gulls flew about screaming to each other in amazement. They had never seen a fire on the water be-fore. That night as the gulls settled down on their rocks, they wondered what would happen next. This was the first time that white men had been left helpless on shore with no ship to carry them home. What would the Indians do? Would they attack the white men and kill them?

But the Indians did nothing of the sort. They brought the sailors food. They helped them to hunt and to fish. So Block and his men lived safely through the winter on Manhattan, probably the first white men to winter there. They saved what they could from the hull of *The Tiger*. They started making a new ship. There was plenty of good timber to be had, but few tools and nails. But by spring a small, new boat was finished. She danced gaily upon the water. *The Restless,* Block named her.

The Restless was an excellent little ship, but she was too small to cross the ocean. Block and his men began to explore along the shore. Up the East River sailed the lit-tle *Restless.* She sailed past the rocks where the sea gulls lived. She sailed past wooded islands. No tall buildings lined the shores. No great bridges spanned the water. No tugboats chugged past.

"Watch out!" screamed the sea gulls. "Swift waters ahead!"

For the East River is not really a river at all. It is a strait that leads from the harbor to Long Island Sound. At the turn in the channel the water is swift and dangerous particularly when the tide is turning. The Indian canoes were often caught and swirled round and round in the whirlpool.

"Watch out!" screamed the sea gulls.

The little *Restless* dipped and ducked. Water broke over her bow. But the wind was behind her. The tide was high. Safely she passed through the dangerous passage. Block named it Hellgate, and so it is called to this day.

With Hellgate safely passed, the water widened out into Long Island Sound. Then the men saw that they were back on the ocean again. They had sailed around the end of Long Island.

The little *Restless* was very useful. She went poking into bays and sailed up rivers for she could go in shallow water. Up the Connecticut River she went and into Narragansett Bay. Block made maps of everything that he saw.

Suddenly across the blue water, a sail appeared. The sailors on the little *Restless* watched it anxiously. The sea was full of pirates. Was this ship friend or foe? Then the sailors recognized the Dutch flag. A loud cheer went up. Another trading ship had arrived from home. Block and his friends climbed quickly aboard the larger ship. They were eager for news.

Back to Holland they sailed. They left the little *Restless*

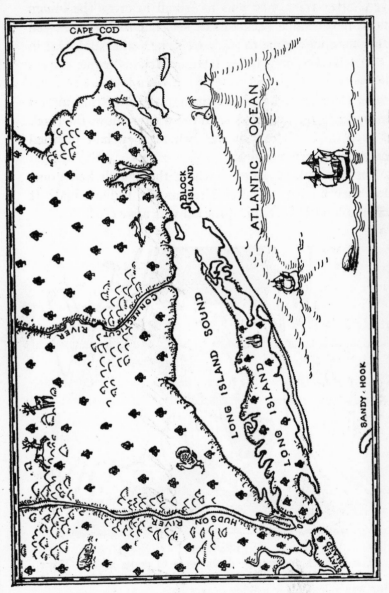

MAP OF THE LAND AND WATERS AROUND MANHATTAN ISLAND

Do you see the strait through which Block sailed "The Restless" into Long Island Sound? Do you see the river that Hudson explored?

for shorter trips. She was too small to cross the ocean. Block never came back to sail her, but his maps helped other men who came to trade in New Netherland. Out in Long Island Sound, Block Island bears his name.

The trading huts on Manhattan were left empty for a while. Deer peered at them through the forest. Squirrels scampered over their roofs. In the winter snow, the track of wolf and wildcat showed where they had prowled about the deserted cabins.

The sea gulls wondered where the Dutch had gone. Had they no wives and children as the Indians had? It was not long before this question was answered.

BEAVERS

The beavers are cutting down trees to make a dam. There were many of them in the swamps on Manhattan Island. Their fur was valuable for making beaver hats.

Chapter Six

THE FIRST SETTLERS

ONE day in 1624 a larger ship arrived than any that had come before. She carried thirty families of fathers, mothers, and children. These people were colonists. Now colonists are people who settle in a new land to stay. Explorers come to find out new routes. Traders come to buy and sell and then go home again. Colonists come to build new homes.

The Indians and the sea gulls gathered to see these pale-faced women and children. They were very much interested. Some of the people talked French, for some of the colonists were Walloons, or French people who had fled to Holland as the Pilgrims had done. In those days not everyone was allowed to worship God as he wished in France, and in many other countries too.

The people were very glad to see shore. They had left Amsterdam in March. Now it was spring and Maytime when they landed. They were very tired of the crowded ship, and of eating salt meat and hard biscuit. Many people had been ill. Storms had tossed the ship. The sailors had kept a sharp lookout for pirates. But now they were safe in harbor with the sea gulls crying a welcome.

The Indian squaws were very surprised to see how the Dutch women dressed. They did not wear deerskin. They wore full gay skirts and white collars. They had white caps on their heads. The pink-cheeked Dutch children clattered about the deck in wooden shoes.

It takes money to send out colonists to settle new land. They need ships to carry them across the sea. They need tools to build houses. They need food to eat while they get their farms started. Over in Holland a company had been started to send out colonists to New Netherland. It was called the Dutch West India Company.

People form a *company* when they get together and put their money into some undertaking. The *company* may build ships for trading, or they may build a factory to make something. Whatever money is made by the ships or the factory is divided up among the people who formed the company. So the Dutch West India Company planned to make money by starting a colony in the New World. It planned to sell the colonists what they needed as soon as they were able to pay. It planned to ship great loads of furs back to Holland to sell.

The Dutch West India Company had other ways of making money. Its ships sometimes lay in wait for Spanish treasure ships from South America laden with gold. One year the Dutch ships captured a whole Spanish fleet. Great was the wealth that went to Amsterdam that fine year! The Dutch West India Company had many other interests besides its colony in New Netherland.

Some of the thirty families that landed sailed up the Great River. A few sailed south to the Delaware River which the Dutch had already explored. Eight men landed on Manhattan. But more people were soon to come. The next year four more shiploads of people arrived. Then came ships carrying "an extraordinary cargo." The sea gulls were more surprised than ever. The passengers on these ships were cows, horses, pigs, and sheep.

Great care had been taken to bring the animals safely across the sea. The decks of the ships had been covered with clean white sand. Below the decks were great tanks of water for the animals to drink. The animals had scarcely known that they were not standing in their own clean Dutch stables, such tender care was taken of them. Only two animals were lost on the whole trip.

The animals were landed on Governors Island, or Nutten Island as the Dutch called it. The men were afraid to take them to Manhattan lest they stray into the woods and be eaten by wolves. There was great excitement as the animals were unloaded. There was baa-ing of sheep, and mooing of cows, and squealing of pigs. Never had the sea gulls heard such a racket.

At last all were safe ashore. The sheep huddled together. The horses galloped around. But soon quiet settled down. The women milked the cows. Men rode the horses. The Indians and the sea gulls were amazed, for the Indians had no tame animals before the white man came. There were, by chance, no wild animals in this country that were good to tame. So the Indians had only their dogs, and the sea gulls considered them worse than useless.

There was not enough grass on Governors Island. The animals had to be ferried across to Manhattan. There something terrible happened. Twenty cows ate a poisonous weed and died. There was grief and sorrow among the people. But enough were left to stock the new farms. Soon Dutch housewives were setting big pans of milk to let the rich, yellow cream rise to the top. They were making big, round cheeses. They were shearing wool to knit warm socks and weave cloth.

The sea gulls were amused at the amount of clothes the Dutch wore. "Why don't they grow feathers as we do, and be done with so much weaving and sewing and washing?" they wondered.

The sea gulls watched the Dutch through the long winter, but when spring came they flew North for nesting. As they flew they saw several other tiny towns being started in the midst of the vast forests. To the north of New Netherland, there was an English town named Plymouth. The people were having a very hard time. More than half their people had died the first winter.

Still farther north on the Saint Lawrence River were French colonists at Quebec. Gulls from farther south reported another English town at Jamestown. Many had died there of starvation and illness. Indians had killed many.

Still farther south, were Spanish towns. Saint Augustine had been started over fifty years before Plymouth or New Amsterdam.

"Dutch, English, Spanish, and French people," wondered the sea gulls. "Why do so many different kinds of people come way across the ocean to this country? What will happen to the Indians? Will all these people live together in peace?"

"I doubt it," said an old black-backed gull who had seen something of the world.

Chapter Seven

THE DUTCH BUY MANHATTAN

IT WAS in the year 1626 that the Dutch West India Company sent over Peter Minuit as governor of New Netherland. Minuit was to make what laws were needed and to manage the affairs for the company. The colonists were to have very little to say about how things were to be run.

The new governor arrived on the good ship, *Sea Mew*. Now sea mew is another name for sea gull. The gulls were very pleased to have the governor arrive on a ship named for them.

One of the first things that Minuit did was to buy the Island of Manhattan from the Indians. For beads and ornaments, bright colored cloth and blankets, knives and axes Peter Minuit "bought the island of Manhattan from the wild men," so the old report says. The goods were worth about sixty guilders in the Dutch money of that day, or twenty-four dollars in our money. Today twenty-four dollars would buy only enough land on Manhattan for a sea gull to perch upon, but neither Minuit nor the Indians knew that in 1626. Minuit paid what seemed to all a fair price.

Soon thirty rough plank houses were built. Then men began a larger building of stone with a thatched roof. It was the storehouse for the Dutch West India Company. Then a mill was built for grinding flour. In a big room above the mill, church services were held.

Nearby, men were busy building a strange walled-in place of logs and dirt and stone. The sea gulls laughed at walls, and they flew over the top to see what was going on. Then they noticed black iron logs at the corners. Cannon! The gulls flew back to the East River.

The sea gulls hated cannon and the noise they made, but the people felt safer. They were afraid of the Indians. They were also afraid of their English neighbors, for the English did not like to have a Dutch colony between their own towns at Plymouth and Jamestown.

The new fort was called Fort Amsterdam, and the little town around the fort was called New Amsterdam. It is pleasant to hear familiar names when you are far from home.

The next thing that the Dutch built surprised the sea gulls more than the fort. It stood up like a great tree with four branches. When the wind blew, the branches swung round and round. If a sea gull flew too near, he was hit and badly hurt. The Indians did not like the big thing any better than the gulls. They said that it "had long arms and teeth that bit the corn to pieces." But the Dutch liked to watch the sails of the windmill turn. The millstones ground their corn to meal. It seemed quite like home.

Each year more people came to New Netherland. Some rich men called Patroons, took up big stretches of land along the Great River and on Staten Island. They paid colonists to come over to help clear their land and start farms.

More houses were built. At first brick and tile were brought from Holland, but soon good clay for bricks was found near. Many of the houses were built with the pointed or gable end of the roof toward the street. The gable ends went up in steps.

Behind the houses, gay gardens soon bloomed. Tulip bulbs had been brought from Holland. Roses, lilies, and violets grew well. In the vegetable gardens there were rows of cabbages, carrots, beets, beans, onions, peas, and many kinds of greens and salads. There was also tobacco which the white man had learned to grow from the Indians. Orchards of fruit trees were soon set out: apple, peach, plum, and cherry trees.

Often tall dark Indians came into the little town to see what the pale-faced women were doing. The Dutch women thought the Indian women dirty and smelly for the Indians rubbed bear grease on their faces to keep off the mosquitoes. The Indian women could see no reason why the Dutch women scrubbed their floors each day, and washed so many clothes. They saw no reason for boiling great kettles of fats to make soap. They saw no reason for spinning and weaving cloth. They tanned deerskin for their clothes until it was as soft as silk. But for all their different ideas, the Dutch and the Indians lived at peace for many years.

The Indian men were willing to hunt and trade with the white men, but few Indians were willing to work for them. There was great need of laborers with so much to be done. Some Negro workmen were sent over. They were a great help. Soon some of them owned homes of their own.

A bakery was built, and a brewery, for the Dutchmen did not want to be without their beer. The fort was made larger, and a tall flag pole was erected. When a ship was sighted coming through the Narrows, the flag was raised. It was the orange, white, and blue flag of the Netherlands with the letters G W C upon it. The letters stand for the Dutch words that mean Dutch West India Company. They are *Geoctroiuyeerde West-Indische Compagnie*. No sea gull has even been able to pronounce that and I doubt if you can.

Although the insides of the little Dutch houses were very clean with their shining brass and copper and silver, outside the streets were far from neat. People threw their rubbish out the front door. Cows and pigs and goats ran through the lanes. The animals were even trampling down the fort.

The governor ordered the farmers to fence in their animals. He ordered the fort repaired. But it was not long before pigs grunted in the mud again. The fort began tumbling down. The sea gulls never did think much of Fort Amsterdam.

People had begun to settle on Long Island. Soon a ferry was started between the village of Breuckelen and Manhattan. On a tree near the shore hung a horn. When a passenger wished to cross, he blew on the horn. The ferryman left his plowing, or whatever he was doing, and rowed the man across. The trip cost six wampum beads.

It was hard to get Dutch money so far from Holland. The colonists soon found it convenient to use Indian wampum. Three wampum beads were worth a stiver, or two cents. For large sums, beaver skins were used. A beaver skin was worth four or five dollars. A good house rented for fifteen beaver skins a year.

It all amused the sea gulls very much. They could fly back and forth between Breuckelen and Manhattan in half the time it took the ferry.

NEW AMSTERDAM

Down at the tip end of Manhattan stood Fort Amsterdam with the little Dutch houses gathered about it. Dutch boats lay at anchor while they were loaded with furs to take to Holland. Indians came to trade in their canoes.

(From the Hartger View)

DUTCH COTTAGE ON BEAVER STREET
Notice the Dutch door divided in the middle, and the thatched roof.
(From an old print in Valentine's Manual)

Chapter Eight

TROUBLE WITH THE INDIANS

AFTER a few years the sea gulls became so used to ships in the harbor that they ceased to wonder at them. Young sea gulls grew up who had never known Manhattan when there were no Dutch houses there, no fort, no windmill.

But the next few years were far from dull. Things went so badly that there was danger that the Dutch people and their houses and their fields would disappear, and the forest return. Things went so badly that the people wrote to the Dutch West India Company and begged for soldiers to fight for them, or ships to carry them all back to Holland. But the company paid little attention to their cries for help.

At first the Indians and the white people had lived peacefully together. There had been disputes, but for the most part "the Indians have lived as lambs among us," the people wrote. But the lambs were to turn to howling wolves.

It was partly due to different ideas about what was right and what was wrong. For instance if a man was killed, the Indians felt that his family must revenge his death. They must kill some one from the tribe that had done the evil deed.

But the Dutch felt quite differently about the matter. They felt that the murderer himself should be punished, not just any member of his clan or tribe.

"But," said the Indians, "if a man does evil, it is the fault of his people. They should have trained their young men better. They must suffer for the guilty one."

"There may be something in that," thought the sea gulls.

Now, in every flock of sea gulls, there are always a few who make trouble. In every group of people, there are always a few foolish ones. This is the sort of thing that happened.

One day while Minuit was governor, three of his servants met an Indian man and boy in the woods beyond the town near the Collect Pond. The Indians carried furs that were worth much money. There was no one to see what happened. The white men fell upon the Indian. They killed him and stole the furs. The Indian boy slipped unseen into the woods.

They say that an Indian never forgets a kindness and never forgives a wrong. Sixteen years later the boy had grown to be a warrior. He came, one day, to the house of an old man who lived near Turtle Bay where the United Nations Building rises today. He asked the old man for cloth to trade. The man bent over a chest to get what was needed, and the Indian struck him dead with his club.

The Dutch people were horrified. They demanded that the Indians punish the young brave, but when the Indian chiefs listened to the whole story they did not feel that he had done wrong. An Indian had been killed treacherously. Now a white man had been killed to even up the sad affair.

Other troubles between the Dutch and Indians came from trading. To get furs cheap, some of the Dutch would sell the Indians rum. Now the Indians were not used to strong drink. It made them drunk and they did not know what they did. The chiefs begged the white men not to sell liquor to their young men. Laws were made forbidding it, but there were always a few greedy white men who would do it. There was no one to watch what happened deep in the woods.

It was the same with guns and ammunition. The Indians wanted guns, but they were far more dangerous to the white men if they were armed with guns. Bullets went farther than arrows. The governor forbade the sale of guns and ammunition to the Indians but, each year, more red men had guns of their own. It was hard to find out how they got them. Fair and honest people must be forever on guard, or wicked, silly people will make trouble for everyone. It was true in New Amsterdam, and it is true today.

Minuit went back to Holland and a new governor named Kieft came to New Amsterdam. Minuit had been just and kind in his dealings with the Indians, but with Kieft it was a different story. Kieft was far from wise. First he decided that the Indians still living on Manhattan must pay part of their corn and furs as a tax to repair the fort. The Indians were furious. What good did the fort do them? Their enemies, the Mohawk Indians from up the Great River, might kill them all and the Dutch soldiers would not stir from the fort to help. The Indians grumbled that the Dutch were taking more and more of their land as well.

Kieft became frightened. He told the men of the town to choose twelve of their number to meet with him and advise him. It was the first time that the people of New Amsterdam had been given a chance to say how their town was to be managed. When people have freedom to discuss how things shall be done, and to vote, we call it a democratic way of governing. This was the first time that democracy had been tried in New Amsterdam. But it did not amount to much. The twelve men did not approve of Kieft's plan, but he went ahead and did what he wanted to anyway.

Kieft's plan was to attack the Indians. He wanted to kill or drive away all the Indians that were left in that part of the country. One of the twelve men was named Peter de Vries. He knew many Indians well, and he went among them and talked their language. He was horrified at Kieft's mad plan.

"It is your own people that you are murdering," he warned.

But Kieft would not listen. At night he sent his soldiers across the Great River. They attacked an Indian village. The soldiers fell upon the sleeping people. Perhaps they did more than Kieft meant them to do. Men, women, and children were killed without mercy.

With a heavy heart, de Vries was sitting by the fire in the governor's house inside Fort Amsterdam. Suddenly he heard shrieks fill the night air. He hurried out to the wall. He could see flames from the burning village.

Suddenly two red men appeared beside him. They had escaped and crossed the river. They thought that it was the Mohawks who had made the sudden attack by night. They had come to the Dutch for help. Sorrowfully de Vries told them the truth. He had no help to offer. The two Indians disappeared into the darkness.

It was not long before the tribes on all sides rose up to carry on the bloody work that Kieft had started. They burned Dutch farmhouses. They killed and carried off prisoners. The Dutch fled to Fort Amsterdam. They crowded inside in terror with what few cows and horses they had been able to save.

Each day brought word of new burnings. The list of dead or missing grew longer. Illness broke out among the people crowded in the fort. Food was scarce. Day and night were filled with misery.

The people complained bitterly to the Dutch West India Company. They said that the fort was more like a mole hill than a fort. They wrote letters complaining of the governor and begging for ships to carry them all back to Holland. But writing letters did not stop the Indians.

From the big farms, or boweries, on Staten Island and along the Great River, from Long Island and Harlem came the same story. One farmhouse on the Harlem

River held out for some time. Its owner had named it the Vale of Peace, but there was little peace there now. Finally a burning arrow set the thatched roof on fire, and the house burned.

That fall, when the sea gulls flew back to Manhattan, they found scarcely a house standing outside the town. The winter was passed "in terror and confusion," the people wrote. It was indeed his own people that Kieft had killed!

INDIAN CANOES

Chapter Nine

THE COUNCIL OF PEACE

IN MARCH of the year 1643, three Indians came to the shore of Long Island. They waved a white flag. They were ready to talk peace.

Kieft called a council in the fort. Who should go over to talk with the red men? Everyone seemed eager to stay in the safety of the fort. No one wished to go, least of all Kieft. Finally two men, Peter de Vries and Jacob Olferz, spoke up. They trusted the faith of the red men. They would go.

The two men crossed the harbor and followed the Indians all day through deep woods. By moonlight, they came to a village of thirty huts. A one-eyed sachem received them. That night the two men slept many miles from Fort Amsterdam, in the midst of a band of red men.

At daybreak they were wakened and led to a place where sixteen chiefs sat in a circle. De Vries and Olferz were placed in the center. Then the talk began. The Indians spoke well for they were trained from boyhood.

One chief held a bundle of little sticks. As he made a point he laid down one stick. When the Dutch had first come to this country, he said, they had often been without food. Had the Indians let them starve? No. They had given their white brothers corn and beans. They had helped them fish and hunt. What had been the Indians' reward? The white men had attacked and killed them. The Indian laid one stick upon the ground.

The white men had often sailed away and left a few of their men behind. What had the Indian done? Had he attacked the helpless few and killed them? No. He had treated the white men as brothers. The Indian laid down another stick.

Now de Vries knew all too well that what the chief said was true. But the chief held many sticks in his hand. The warriors were beginning to mutter angrily at the memory of their wrongs. De Vries could not see that it was going to do any good to talk the matter all over.

So de Vries spoke to the council. He said that all the chief told was true. The white man had acted foolishly and cruelly. But now the thing to do was to make peace so that both peoples could get to their spring planting. Would the chiefs come with him to the fort to receive gifts from Kieft?

The Indians hesitated. Was this a trick to trap their leaders in the fort? De Vries gave his word that they would be safe. At last a solemn procession marched down to the shore. While they waited for the tide to come in, a messenger came darting through the woods. He brought a message from a distant chief.

"Do not trust the Dutch," warned the runner. "When the chiefs are in the fort at the mercy of the Dutch, they will turn upon them and kill them. The tribes will be helpless without their leaders." The messenger begged the chiefs to turn back.

The Indians looked at de Vries. All he could do was to promise them safety. One old chief spoke up. He said that de Vries was different from the other Dutch. Never had he known de Vries to lie. "We will go," said the chief, "on the faith of your word."

Eighteen Indians and the two white men climbed into a dugout canoe. The boat settled into the water to within a handbreadth of its edge. The gulls flew about and screamed with surprise. Across the harbor went the canoe to Manhattan.

The sachems followed de Vries through the little town. People watched them fearfully. Children hid behind their mothers' skirts. Men thought of their dead friends and burned homes. In the fort, Kieft gave presents to the Indians. The white men and the red smoked the pipe of peace together. Then back to their woodland homes went the sachems in safety.

But as usual Kieft did the wrong thing. He should have paid dearly for the harm that he had done. But he was foolish. The Indians grumbled at the poor presents that he had given them. They thought of their women and children who had been butchered by the Dutch. In a few months there were new complaints of Indian attacks.

De Vries did his best. He went into the forest to buy back a young Dutch boy who had been taken prisoner. He saved the lives of two Indians who had come into the town on a peaceful errand, and who were threatened by a crowd of angry people. It seemed hopeless to keep the peace. De Vries gave up and went home to Holland.

But, at last, the Dutch West India Company sent over a hundred and twenty soldiers. The English in New England were fighting the Indians too. At last the red man saw that there was nothing that he could do but make peace. Again the peace pipe was smoked in Fort Amsterdam. The Indians buried their tomahawks in the ground. The Indians promised not to come armed near a white man's house. The white men promised not to enter an Indian village without permission. And a little white girl who had been taken prisoner was to be returned.

The little eight-year-old girl was the daughter of Anne Hutchinson, an English woman who had been driven out of Boston because of her beliefs. She had a big farm near Pelham Bay Park. She and sixteen of her family had been scalped by the Indians. The little girl alone remained alive. She had been a prisoner for two years. She had forgotten her own language and she wept when she left her captors who had been kind to her. Today the Hutchinson River Parkway bears that family's name.

Scalpings and burnings were over for a time. The old writings say that peace was made, "in the fort under the blue canopy of heaven." The next day was set for "Thanksgiving for the long desired peace."

There were not many people left on Manhattan. Those who lived outside the town went sadly back to build up their ruined farms. But the Dutch West India Company decided that things were going badly in New Netherland. Fighting Indians was not making anyone rich. One man named Van der Donck went over to Holland with a report on how matters stood. A new governor was sent out. Kieft was ordered home.

So away sailed Kieft. Some good things had been done for the town during his stay. An inn, the highest building in New Amsterdam, stood five stories high by the East River. Inside the fort a church had been built. The minister, or domine as he was called, had preached against Kieft's evil ways, and Kieft had ordered his soldiers to beat on drums and play noisy games outside the church so the people could not hear the sermon. But even firing off guns could not stop the domine. He kept right on preaching just the same.

Kieft never reached Holland. His ship was wrecked off the coast of England. A few men swam ashore, but Kieft and eighty others drowned.

NEW AMSTERDAM IN 1655

The town has grown larger but the little houses still huddle around the fort. Can you see
the governor's house and the church of Saint Nicholas inside the wall?

(From the Iconography of Manhattan Island, by I. N. Phelps Stokes)

Chapter Ten

The New Governor Arrives

ON MAY 11, in 1647, the new governor arrived. His wife was with him. Cloppety, cloppety, clop he stamped along. His right leg was made of wood bound with silver bands. His name was Peter Stuyvesant. He had been governor of one of the islands in the West Indies, and he had lost his leg fighting for his country.

Stuyvesant looked about the little town with a firm glance. About seven hundred people were living in the hundred and twenty houses. Dirt lanes twisted from house to house. When it was dry, they were dusty. When it rained, they were deep in mud. Rubbish was thrown out into them in a most untidy manner. Pigs rooted where they wished. Cows, chickens, and geese wandered at will. Fort Amsterdam as usual was tumbling down.

The new governor decided to do his best to make the town a better place. He decided to do so whether the people wished it or not. He gave the people a long talk.

"I will govern you," he said, "as a father governs his children."

But the people were not children. They did not like to be told just what they must do. It made no difference whether Stuyvesant's ideas were good or bad. They did not like to be ordered about. Stuyvesant was an old soldier and he was used to giving orders. He had a violent temper. He lost it about the time he came to New Netherland, and there is no record of his finding it again until he went to live on his farm by the East River and another man came to govern the town.

Stuyvesant began to issue orders. People must not play noisy games, or fight, or buy drink during church time. Ugly fences, tumble-down pigpens, old sheds must come down. New buildings must be well placed to improve the looks of the town. Rubbish and garbage must be carted away. The fort must be repaired. Pigs and cows must be kept at home. And so on and on the orders went.

The town began to look better. Seventeen streets were laid out and some were paved with cobblestones. Mrs. Olaf van Cortlandt was said to be the first housewife to get the street paved before her door, because she complained bitterly of the mud tracked in on her clean floor.

A wharf was built. That was a great improvement. Before that, large ships had anchored in the bay while their cargoes were sent ashore in barges. A wharf, where ships could unload, saved much time and labor.

At first Stuyvesant lived in the governor's house inside the fort. There his two small sons, Balthazar and Nicholas, were born. Later he built himself a fine new house of white stone. Its garden ran down to the water front. Outside the town, he bought a country place which was called the Bowery.

Then Stuyvesant had something else built that amused the sea gulls as much as the fort did. He had a great wall built right across the end of Manhattan Island. There had been a fence there before to keep the cattle from straying, but now Stuyvesant had a wall built nine planks high. The sea gulls flew back and forth over it, but people could only come in through the two gates.

The wall was for protection. There was still danger from the Indians. Once when Stuyvesant was away at a Dutch fort on the Delaware River, a thousand Indians had swarmed through the streets of New Amsterdam. Hundreds of canoes lined the shore. People huddled in their houses in terror. Stuyvesant came hurrying back. The people in New Amsterdam were safe, but a hundred had been killed on Staten Island and the mainland.

But there were other enemies beside Indians. The English had never liked having the Dutch hold the land between New England and Virginia. Indeed some of the English said that the Dutch had no right to any part of America. There were quarrels about land on Long Island and along the Connecticut River. With all this trouble, Stuyvesant knew too well that his little town needed protection.

So a wall, too high for Indians to climb, was built from the East River to the Great River. All that there was of the town lay to the south of it. Through one of the two gates each morning, the town herdsman drove the cattle to pasture. Loud and clear his horn sounded through the lanes. Out hurried the cows from the barns. At the end of the day, home they came to be milked, and each cow knew her own barn. Then the gates in the wall were closed and locked, and a guard set.

Still other dangers Stuyvesant guarded against. The

worst of these was fire. Houses stood close together. Many roofs were thatched with reeds. Some chimneys were made of logs covered with clay instead of brick or stone. Barns and haystacks stood near houses.

Now and again a family would be sitting near a blazing fire in the fireplace of a winter's evening. The mother would be knitting. With stockings for all the family to knit, her fingers were never idle. The father might be smoking and telling the children stories about the blue and white tiles around the fireplace. Each tile had a picture on it, and each picture, a story.

Perhaps the chimney became too hot. Perhaps sparks fell on the thatched roof. Suddenly the cry of "FIRE," would pierce the night. Out would rush the frightened family. Neighbors would come running to help. As much as possible would be saved. The featherbeds would be snatched from the cupboard beds built against the wall. The cradle would be carried out. The precious chairs with the red leather seats, brought from Holland, would be saved. If possible the great *kas,* or chest filled with linen, would be carried out. There was not much that could be done to save the house.

Another time it might be the haystack by the barn that caused the trouble. There were no matches in those days. Getting a spark with flint and steel was slow work on a cold morning. At night, housewives covered the red coals in their fireplaces with ashes. But sometimes in the morning the coals had gone out. The housewife would snatch up a shovel and run to a neighbor to borrow some fire. Perhaps as she ran home, she was careless and let some red ashes fall. A wisp of hay might catch, then the haystack, then the barn and house.

Stuyvesant began to issue more orders. No man should

have a wooden chimney. All chimneys should be inspected, for clean chimneys were less likely to catch fire than ones full of soot. No more haystacks near houses. If any man had a fire, he had to pay a fine as well as lose his house.

The governor ordered one hundred and fifty fire buckets to be made. Who should make them? It would take over a year to get them from Holland. The shoemakers of the town were called together. Would they make them of leather? They would, and each citizen of the town was taxed a beaver skin to pay for them.

The leather buckets were placed at convenient spots. At the cry of "FIRE," men grabbed them. They formed a double line from the nearest well or brook to the house. The buckets were swung from man to man, down the line, and the water hurled on the burning house. Then back went the empty ones for more water.

People felt safer. They could sleep more peacefully at night now, too, for a night watchman went the rounds of the town after sunset. He carried a lantern with a candle burning in it, a rattle to scare away thieves, a stout staff, and an hourglass to tell the time.

The sea gulls often heard him call across the water: "Ten o'clock of a fair night and all's well."

PLAN OF NEW AMSTERDAM

Can you find Fort Amsterdam? The church of Saint
Nicholas in the fort? The grass plot which is now Bowling
Green? The wall that Stuyvesant built across the island?
There were two gates in the wall, one at Broadway and one

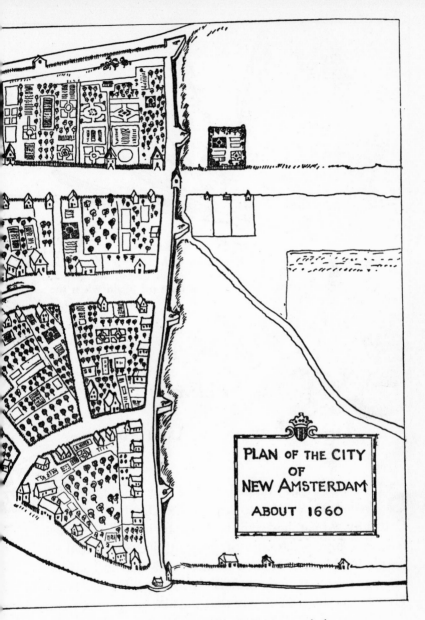

at the East River. Can you find them? Stuyvesant's house was
on the East River near the harbor. It was a large house with
a garden. Can you find it? Can you find the Grand Canal?
Can you find the Dutch windmill? What do you think this
part of town looks like today?

(From the Iconography of Manhattan Island, by I. N. Phelps Stokes)

QUILL PENS, INK AND SAND

Quill pens were cut from feathers with a sharp little knife called a pen-knife. Sand was used instead of blotting paper. It was poured over the wet ink, and then off again when the ink was dry.

Chapter Eleven

THE CITY OF NEW AMSTERDAM

STUYVESANT needed money for the town. He needed money also to send to the Dutch West India Company which had not been capturing any Spanish treasure ships of late. So Stuyvesant, like Kieft, told the people to choose nine men to meet with him to help him manage the town, and particularly to help him raise taxes. He was very careful to say that the nine men should only meet when he called them together. He did not want anyone to interfere with him.

But the nine men had ideas of their own, and they soon

did interfere, or at least try to. Stuyvesant lost his temper at them.

"Clowns, rascals, liars, and rebels!" he shouted as he stamped up and down the council room on his wooden leg.

The nine men complained to the company about Stuyvesant. "The English towns in America are getting on better than the Dutch," they said. "The taxes in New Netherland are too high. We pay a tax on the furs we send to Holland. We pay taxes on the things we buy. With taxes here and taxes there we have little left for ourselves. And we are not allowed to say how the money is to be spent. We cannot even elect our officers as people do in Holland."

In Holland it was quite different. Each city in Holland chose a *schout* and *burgomasters* and *schepens*. These men made the laws that had to do with the city. They were the judges if anyone broke the laws. They attended to many things that our police attend to now. If the people did not think their officers were fair and honest, they could choose new ones at the next election. The people of New Amsterdam begged that they might be governed as the cities of Holland were governed.

At last word came back from the Dutch West India Company that it would be as the people wished. New Amsterdam should become a city. It should have a seal and it should choose its own officers. But there was one difficulty. The company forgot to say just who should do the choosing.

"We are the ones," cried the leading people of the new city. "That is the way it is in Holland."

But Stuyvesant said that he was the one to choose, and

that was quite a different matter. People objected, but Stuyvesant was not one to listen to objections.

Then people from the Dutch towns on Long Island, and from Flushing and Gravesend, met with the leading men of New Amsterdam, and they sent a petition to Holland asking for their rights. But Stuyvesant said that, if everyone was allowed to vote, thieves would vote for thieves, and rascals for rascals, and then where would they all be? He sent his soldiers to break up the meetings.

"Go to your homes," they ordered.

The disputes went on for six years. At last Stuyvesant had to give in. Only well-to-do men of the town, or burghers as they were called, could hold office. The inn that had been built in Kieft's day was turned into a city hall and was called the *stadt huys*. Here the new officers of the city met, and here Stuyvesant lost his temper.

When there was a notice to give to the people, the bell on the stadt huys rang. Ding, dong, ding went the bell.

"Come on," cried all the people as they gathered quickly to hear the news, for there were no newspapers or radio in those days. The notice was read aloud, and then posted on the wall for those who could to read it.

Stuyvesant and the officers met of a Sunday morning at the stadt huys, and marched in a solemn procession to the church of Saint Nicholas, inside the old fort. A servant went ahead, and carried cushions for the worthies to sit upon.

It must have been pleasant to have cushions to sit on, for the wooden benches in the church were hard. The sermons were two hours long! Very long indeed they seemed to the Dutch boys and girls.

"Oh dear," sighed the little girls as they sat primly by their mothers.

THE STADT HUYS
(From an old print)

"Oh dear," sighed the boys as they marched into church together under the eye of the schoolmaster who led the singing.

At school the master had taught the children prayers and psalms and the catechism. Much of the school time was spent on these matters. But the children were "instructed in reading and writing and also in the fear of the Lord," from eight until eleven o'clock, and from one till four. Only boys were taught arithmetic.

Beginners learned to read from a big A B C book with the picture of a cock on it. Writing was done with pens cut from quills. The schoolmaster ground the ink from a solid cake and mixed it with water. On his desk lay a paddle to punish bad children, and an oil can to oil the clock hanging on the wall. Parents paid for their children's schooling in beaver skins, but "the poor who came asking in the name of the Lord were taught for nothing."

Once a week the children were tested on their catechisms, and upon what the minister had said in his sermon, so boys and girls sat as still as they could in church, and listened. Now and again in winter came the scratching sound of a foot stove being pushed over the sanded floor from one member of the family to another. There was no heat in church. Toes ached with the cold. The little stove full of hot ashes was welcome. Everyone wanted a turn at it.

After the service the families walked home to their cozy, clean little houses. The fathers were in knee breeches and wide white collars, wide brimmed hats and long capes. The women had full skirts and short jackets. Their white collars and caps were often of finest linen with lace and embroidery upon them. The women looked as gay and bright as their own flower beds in spring.

A DUTCH FAMILY MEAL 17th CENTURY

(From an old print in Singleton's Dutch New York)

The little girls were dressed like their mothers. The boys dressed like their fathers. They looked like little men and women as they walked sedately home from church.

At other times they were not as sedate as they flew over the ice on their skates, or slid down hill on home-made sleds, or played ball, or teased the night watchman by shouting "Indians!" But the best fun of the year was the kermis, or fair, in August, when there were jugglers and puppet shows to watch, dancing bears and trained dogs, and cakes and sweets to eat.

Good dinners awaited the families at home. No one went hungry in a Dutch house if the mother could help it. Big dishes of meat and fish would be placed upon the table. There would be lobsters or oysters from the harbor, and perhaps a turkey, or a haunch of venison bought from the Indians and roasted on a spit in front of the great kitchen fire. It was fresh meat or fish if that could be had. Otherwise it was salted and taken from the big barrels of brine in the cellar.

Not only the cellar in every house, but also the attic was a storage place for food. In those days there was no corner store to run to for a bit of this or a bit of that as there is today. There were no deep freezes and cold stor-age plants, no refrigerator cars to whisk across the coun-try with fresh meat and fruits and vegetables. There were no canneries to put up food in tin cans ready for use at any time. The housewife must have her storeroom well stocked with salted and smoked meat and fish, buckets of sausage meat, piles of carrots, beets, onions, and cabbages banked in earth, and for desserts, baskets of dried apples and peaches and cherries, homemade jellies and preserves.

On special days there were special dishes served. On St. Martin's day everyone must have a well-roasted goose.

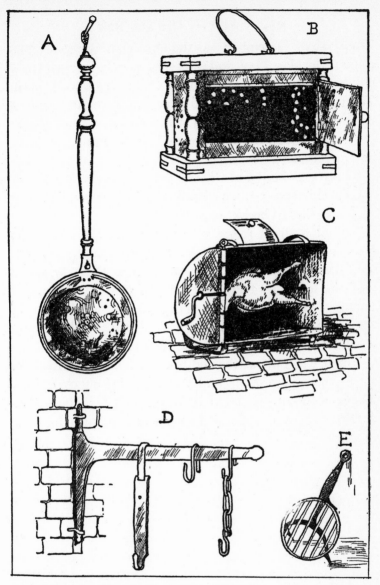

A. Warming Pan. B. Foot Stove. Hot ashes or charcoal were put in the warming pan and the foot stove. C. Spit. By turning the handle the meat was roasted on both sides. D. Pothooks. They held the kettles over the fire. E. Trivet. It was set in the hot ashes to hold dishes that were to be kept warm.

The sixth of December was the Dutch Christmas. It was Saint Nicholas Day and presents were given to good children, but a bad child found a whip in his wooden shoe. Then there were waffles and pancakes, tarts and almond cookies. On New Year's Day, when everyone went calling on their friends, the tables were loaded with fried cakes and sweetmeats.

There was beer and wine to drink at every meal, milk for the children. Tea was drunk of an afternoon, but beer took the place of breakfast coffee.

"What a great many different things the Dutch do have to eat," wondered the sea gulls who kept largely to fish themselves. "And how much time they do spend working to get it. They have oxen to plow for them, and horses to draw their carts. They use the wind to grind their meal and blow their ships. And still they have even less time to themselves than the Indians had!"

For it was only at the end of a busy day that the men sat by their door-stoops and smoked their long clay pipes. The women knitted and visited with their neighbors. The children played games together. The sea gulls had far more leisure.

Chapter Twelve

THE YEAR 1664

"FOUR ships well-armed and they fly the English flag," cried a kittiwake gull who came flying in from the outer bay. The sea gulls knew the English flag well. More and more English were settling in this country. The English colonies were growing faster than the Dutch.

When news of the approaching ships reached the people of New Amsterdam, they were horrified. Stuyvesant was at Fort Orange up the Great River. A messenger was sent for him. Home he hurried by boat. Boats were the fastest way to travel in those days of poor roads, or no roads.

As usual Fort Amsterdam was tumbling down. The wall across the island was tumbling down. There were few soldiers in the fort and less ammunition. Again and again Stuyvesant had begged the company for more men and money. Little attention had it paid. Now it would expect him to defend the town, and that was easier said than done.

Stuyvesant ordered half the men of the town to report each day with shovels and wheelbarrows to repair the fort. He drilled those who were fit to be soldiers. Then he sent a messenger to the man who was in command of the English ships. Colonel Nicolls was his name. Stuyvesant demanded of Nicolls to know why English ships should sail without permission into Dutch waters. What did the English want?

Back came very unpleasant word from Nicolls. He had been ordered to capture New Amsterdam. He called upon Stuyvesant to surrender the town and all of New Netherland to him.

Stuyvesant was aghast. England and Holland were at peace. There was a treaty of friendship between the two countries. But the English king, Charles the Second, was not one to be bound by treaties or promises. He had decided to attack New Netherland.

"Never will I surrender!" cried Stuyvesant.

Nicolls sent back more messages. If the Dutch would give in without fighting, no harm would come to the people. They would be safe and they could stay on in their homes.

Stuyvesant called the leading men of the town together. Now Stuyvesant told these men what Nicolls had offered, but he did not dare tell the townsfolk. He was afraid that if they knew that Nicolls promised them safety, they would be willing to surrender. He was afraid that many people in New Amsterdam did not really much care whether they were ruled by Holland or England.

A second message came from Nicolls. Again he demanded that Stuyvesant surrender, and again he promised safety to the people if they gave in peacefully.

Stuyvesant stamped up and down the council room in

fury. The whole thing was an outrage! Give in? Stuyvesant was an old soldier. He did not care what happened to himself, but fight he would! He was in command of the town. He would defend it from these robbers. Stuyvesant tore up the paper from Nicolls and threw the bits on the floor. If he ordered his people to fight, they must fight to the last man.

But neither the last man nor the first man seemed eager to fight. The Dutch knew they could not drive away the English. What could their few cannon do against four well-armed ships? If the ships' guns were turned on the town, the houses would be destroyed, the people killed. New Amsterdam had nothing to gain and all to lose.

A crowd gathered outside the stadt huys and shouted to know what terms Nicolls had offered. At last Stuyvesant had to give in. His secretary pieced together the torn paper. One of the burgomasters read it aloud. When they heard what it said, men, women, and children begged the governor to give in, but still Stuyvesant refused.

The English grew tired. Two ships sailed through the Narrows and anchored beside the fort. They were so close at hand that the people ashore could see the gunners standing by their cannon. Stuyvesant watched them from the walls of the fort. His few soldiers were near, armed with helmets and breastplates. But they were far from eager to fight.

"What can my lord do?" asked the chief gunner piteously. "He knows well that there is little powder and most of it good for nothing. Were I to commence firing in the morning, I would have no powder left by noon."

The minister of the Dutch Church, good Domine Megapolensis, drew near. "Of what avail are our poor guns against the broadside of more than sixty cannon," he said. "It is wrong to shed blood for no purpose."

Still Stuyvesant hesitated. His duty was his duty. Then a paper was handed him. It was from the people of the town pleading with him to surrender. It was signed by many of the important people. Stuyvesant's face was set in a frown as he looked firmly at it. Then he saw a name that made him pause. His own son, Balthazar, now grown to be a man, had signed. Everyone was against him.

Slowly Stuyvesant turned to his councilors. "Well, let it be so," he said bitterly. "I would much rather have been carried to my grave." Beaten and discouraged, he gave the order to surrender. The dominie led him gently from the hall.

The Dutch and the English met at Stuyvesant's country home, the Bowery, to talk over terms. Two days later the Dutch soldiers marched from the fort. The trumpeter blew his horn. The men carried their guns with fuses lighted ready to fire, to show that they had not been beaten but had given in of their own free will. Then down came the Dutch flag from the fort. It was not the orange, white, and blue one, for a few years before Holland had changed the orange stripe to red as it is today. But New York City still keeps the orange, white, and blue for its beautiful city flag.

The sea gulls screamed a good-by to the soldiers as they sailed away.

Up from the shore marched the English, and up went the English flag. The little town settled down, a Dutch town no longer but an English one.

The name New Amsterdam was changed to New York. The Dutch settlement at Fort Orange was called Albany. All this was because Nicolls had been sent over by the brother of the King of England. His name was James, Duke of York and Albany.

Except for the change of names, the sea gulls could not see that it made much difference who ruled the town. Many English people had been living there. Indeed eighteen different languages could be heard upon the street: Dutch, English, French, German, Yiddish, Spanish, and many others.

One of the reasons that people from so many different countries had come to New Amsterdam was that the Dutch believed in giving people freedom to worship God as they pleased. Those who did not go to the Dutch Church were allowed freedom if they held services quietly in their own homes. It was only the Quakers who were driven out, and some were thrown in prison and beaten. Stuyvesant arrested one Quaker leader from Flushing named John Bowne. He sent him to Amsterdam to be tried. But the Dutch West India Company could see no harm in a man who preached peace and love, and they sent Bowne back, and told Stuyvesant to leave the Quakers alone.

Now that New Amsterdam had become New York, there were both Dutch and English services in the church inside the fort. Dutch and English settled down peacefully together.

"What's in a name anyway?" said the sea gulls.

But there were differences that sea gulls do not understand. Burgomasters, schepens, and schout no longer marched to church. Instead there were a mayor, sheriffs, and aldermen. But the people could no longer choose their officers. The governor alone chose them. The people grumbled, but that was the way the Duke of York had said it should be, and there is no good arguing in the face of battleships.

Nicolls tried to be just. He chose good men, four were Dutch and three English.

"That is all right when we have wise governors," muttered the people. "But what if England sends us bad ones?" And that was a question that would come up again and again in the years ahead.

Stuyvesant was no longer in New York. He sailed back to Holland to be blamed by the Dutch West India Company. Firmly the old man stood his ground. He had not acted from cowardice, but from necessity. His was an "upright and loyal heart," he said. Indeed he went so far as to tell the company that it was really all their fault that they had lost New Netherland.

Then back to New York he came. He lived for many years on his Bowery. Colonel Nicolls often rode out of an afternoon to call.

On his Bowery Stuyvesant died when he was eighty years old. Today near the beautiful old church of St. Mark's-In-The-Bouwerie at Second Avenue and Tenth Street, you can see his grave. The church stands where the chapel stood upon his country place.

But some people say that at twelve o'clock of a New Year's Eve, in the old part of the town, there comes a rattle of ghostly drums. Out stalks the Dutch patrol, and behind them comes a tall dark figure with a wooden leg. Thump, thump, thump he goes through the old streets, to see how his town fares.

Chapter Thirteen

THE POST TO BOSTON

IN A few years Nicolls went back to England. The Duke of York had helped him about as much as the Dutch West India Company had helped Stuyvesant. The people of New York were sorry to see him go. Little did they know that he was soon to be killed by a Dutch cannon ball as he stood by his master, the Duke of York, on the deck of an English warship.

The next governor was named Lovelace. One of the first things he did was to buy Staten Island from the Indians. The Dutch had farmed the island, but the matter of who owned it had never been properly settled. So for "38 coats, 30 shirts, 30 kettles, 20 guns, 30 hoes, and 50 knives" the last of the Indians moved away from Staten Island.

A few Indians still lived at the north end of Manhattan. You can still see the rocks blackened by their campfires in the caves at Inwood Park. But the white men's cattle ruined the Indians' cornfields which were unfenced. Little by little the white man kept taking more of the Indians' land. So the red man gave up his hunting grounds, and Manhattan knew him no more.

Up the Hudson River, as the Great River was now called, the Five Nations of the Iroquois Indians were still powerful. Again and again governors journeyed through the forests to make peace with them. The Indians were strong friends or fierce enemies. The French colonists in Canada tried to turn the Five Nations against the English, but for the most part, the tribes were loyal to "the great sachem across the sea," as they called the king.

Now that New York was English, a mail route was to be started between New York and Boston. The way led through two hundred miles of deep forest.

"Search out a man," ordered the governor, "who is strong, active, and tireless."

Such a man was found. A locked box was placed in the fort to receive letters to go to Boston. On the 22nd of January in 1673, the postman started out on his first trip. Up Broadway he rode and out the gate in Peter Stuyvesant's wall.

Thud, thud, thud went his horse's hoofs on the frozen dirt road. In the spring it would be deep mud. Now it was hard and rutted by the wheels of heavy farm wagons. But it had lately been much improved, and it led all the way to New Harlem, the village at the northern end of Manhattan.

Farms were left behind. The postman rode through swamps where reeds and cattails stuck up through the ice. The higher ground beyond was wooded. Herds of shaggy ponies ran wild. They wondered when they saw one of their kind with a man upon his back. Then they snorted and kicked up their independent heels, and galloped away.

SMIT'S VLY AT THE FOOT OF MAIDEN LANE

The old hunting ground of the Indians has gone. White men are everywhere on Manhattan Island, farming and working. One boat has been drawn out of the water for repairs. The other is just being built. Do you see the well sweep with the bucket hanging from it? Notice also the windmill placed on a hill to catch the breezes.

(From an old print in Valentine's Manual)

In three hours the postman reached Harlem. People rushed out to see who the rider might be. He stopped to rest his horse, and tell his news, and drink a pot of beer in the tavern.

"A post to Boston," cried the people in amazement. "Once every month he will bring letters and news. To think that we should live to see this day!"

Then those who knew how to write went home to try to think of something to say in a letter.

The ferryman took the rider and his horse across the Harlem River. Then off he rode across the land once owned by Jonas Bronk as a farm. It still bears his name. Soon farms and roads were left behind as the rider plunged into heavy forests. He carried a sharp hatchet. As he rode through the woods he marked his way by slashing the bark of tall trees along the way. He crossed rivers on the ice. He slept in log cabins or, if none was at hand, by his own campfire. He listened to the howls of hungry wolves. He saw the tracks of wildcats. Startled deer leaped from the woods.

Back came the postman at the end of the month. He carried his letters to the inn, where they were looked over and talked over by half the town before they reached their owners.

What would that postman have thought if he had known that the day would come when it would take over six thousand postmen to collect and deliver mail in the city of New York? What would he have thought if he had seen the main post office building which covers two city blocks where were once Dutch farms? Chutes underground carry letters from branch post offices to the main one. Six or seven million letters a day are shot underground through them. Trains run under the building, and bags of letters are dropped down to them. Airplanes carry letters to Boston in an hour instead of in two weeks.

Over the General Post Office Building today are carved these words. They were written twenty-five hundred years ago about the runners who carried messages for the Kings of Persia:

Neither snow nor rain nor heat nor gloom of night stays these couriers from the swift completion of their appointed tasks.

Through snow and rain and gloom of night that first postman rode out upon his lonely way.

But it was not for long. Something happened that same year that was very surprising to the sea gulls. Dutch ships came sailing into New York Bay. Dutch sailors marched ashore. A few shots were fired. Then down came the English flag. Up went the Dutch flag.

"This looks like old times," said the sea gulls.

That is what had happened. England and Holland were at war with each other.

"This would be a good time to take back New Netherland," said a Dutch general.

Over came the Dutch ships and took the English by surprise. But instead of calling the town New Amsterdam again, it was named New Orange in honor of William, Prince of Orange who ruled the Netherlands. The fort was repaired. For the first and last time in its history it was really in good repair and had plenty of guns and ammunition.

The guns were never fired. Just then Holland and England made peace. It was decided that England should have New York after all. Down came the Dutch. Up went the English.

It was very confusing to the sea gulls and to a great many people as well.

When the Dutch governor left, he gave his coach to the new English governor. It was the only one in town. Children stopped to stare at it as it rattled over the rough cobblestones of the streets.

OLD WEATHER VANE
(In the New York Historical Museum)

Chapter Fourteen

THE SEAL OF THE CITY OF NEW YORK

THE new English governor passed a law that was important to the city. It was called The Bolting Act. All wheat from the farms around must be brought into New York to be bolted, that is to have the rough outer part sifted from the flour. This meant that all flour must be inspected and packed in barrels and shipped from New York City.

The farmers up the Hudson River grumbled. They could bolt their own wheat and ship it from their own wharves more cheaply. But grumbling did no good.

The Bolting Act was good for trade in New York City. Flour mills were built. Coopers opened up new shops to make barrels to hold all the flour. New bakeries opened to bake the flour into hardtack biscuits which were used for bread on shipboard in those days. More people came to the city and more money was made.

New York began to grow. New streets were laid out. The old canal of Dutch days was filled in and a fine new street built over it. Broad Street it was called. A new and better wharf was built.

Today the seal of New York City tells much of its early history. Two barrels are in memory of this same Bolting Act. Wings from a windmill tell of the old Dutch days. Two beavers tell of the early fur trading when beavers built their dams across the streams on Manhattan Island. A woodland Indian stands at one side and a Dutch sailor at the other. At first there was a crown at the top of the seal to show that the city was ruled by the English king. Later the crown was changed to an eagle—but that is another story.

In a few years in 1683 a new governor came out from England named Dongan. He moved into Stuyvesant's town house and called it Whitehall after the King's palace in London. The name still clings to that part of town, and out on Staten Island, Dongan Hills bears the name of this same man.

Dongan brought good news. King Charles of England had sent New York a charter. Down at the Public Library at Forty-second Street and Fifth Avenue today you can see the Dongan Charter on five great sheets of parchment. It gave the people of New York the right to vote.

But much good did the charter do! Just then King Charles died. His brother, the Duke of York, was crowned king. He was King James the Second. He was the same Duke of York who had sent Nicolls to capture New Amsterdam. He was the man for whom New York is named. He took back the freedom which the Dongan Charter had given to the people. Worse still, he said that New York and New England should be joined together.

The people of New York and the people of New England were furious. But luckily England did not like King James any better than America did. They soon rose up against him and drove him out of England. His daughter, Mary, had married William, Prince of Orange and lived in Holland. The people of England asked her and her husband to come to rule them.

Soon word reached New York that the good Queen Mary and her husband had given back the rights that James had taken away. An election was held and the people of New York voted for the men that should hold office. The city was given a new seal.

The gulls felt that it was too bad that the city was named for such a foolish man as James the Second. Richmond was named for his brother's son. Queens was named for his brother's wife.

"But perhaps those names will remind people," said an old black-bearded gull, "of how much harm bad rulers can do."

THE FIRST SEAL OF NEW YORK CITY

Notice (1) the Indian and the beavers; (2) the wings of the windmill and the flour barrels; (3) the sailor. There is a crown on the seal because New York was ruled by the English king in 1686.

Chapter Fifteen

SMUGGLERS AND PIRATES

FOR some time the sea gulls had noticed mysterious ships that crept into the East River at night. Little boats, heavily laden, rowed ashore in the darkness.

"Why do they unload secretly at night?" asked a young gull.

"Pirates and smugglers," muttered an old gull, and dropped off to sleep again.

England had passed laws that the people in America did not like. If people in America bought goods from any country except England, they must pay high taxes on them. Goods must be brought to the colonies in English ships.

Perhaps Dutch ships carried molasses and sugar from Cuba for less money than English ships did. Perhaps France made better silks and gloves than England. If Americans bought Dutch sugar or fine French gloves, they must pay high taxes. What was worse, people in America were forbidden to make many things for themselves. They could not weave cloth. They must buy their cloth from England. They must not make nails and tools. They must buy them from England. English merchants

OLD HOUSE ON BROAD STREET

New York was still very Dutch in appearance in 1698. Notice
the gable going up in steps. What do you think is in the barrels
and boxes? Perhaps there is molasses or flour in the barrels
and tea in the boxes.

(From an old print in Singleton's Dutch New York)

and shipowners made money, but the Americans hated the laws.

The governors appointed officers to see that the taxes were paid, but these officers often saw less than the sea gulls did. They looked the other way when smugglers brought in goods without paying taxes. Some officers grew rich themselves on bribes paid by the smugglers.

The shops of the little city were filled with fine silks and brocades that had been sent secretly ashore. There were plenty of sugar and spices, and carved furniture and ivory ornaments. The sailors who came ashore were a gay, rollicking lot with plenty of money to spend. The captains wore the finest of velvets and silks and gold lace. Swords hung at their belts and they were handy with their pistols.

These mysterious ships were well armed. The kittiwake gulls told strange tales about them.

A full rigged ship would come sailing merrily along. She was three weeks from port and all went well. Her sailors were pulling on the ropes to put up more sail, and singing a sea chanty as they worked. Suddenly another sail appeared far away.

"Is it friend or foe?" was the question on every lip.

The merchant ship tried to change her course to run past the other ship, but the newcomer was fast. Slowly but surely she gained. There was no escape.

"What flag does she fly?" asked the captain.

"No flag, sir," answered the man in the crow's nest.

"Pirates!" muttered the captain, and he ordered his men to make ready for attack.

All day long under a bright blue sky, the chase went on. By late afternoon as the sun was low, the two ships were near enough for the gunners to fire. It was almost a relief to have something happen after waiting, waiting, waiting all day long. The deck of the merchant ship shuddered as a cannon ball hit it.

Slowly the pirate ship drew near her victim. Her men threw great hooks across to hold the two ships together. Then the pirates swarmed over the sides and onto the other ship. Inch by inch they fought back the sailors. The pirates showed no mercy. Many sailors preferred death to being taken prisoner.

As the sun dropped round and red into the sea, the last sailors surrendered. The cargo of the merchant ship was carried across to the pirate ship. It was a rich cargo. The pirates would be well paid for their day's work. All night they worked under a full moon.

When the merchant ship was empty, the pirates left her. But before they had sailed far, the empty ship burst into flame. They had set her afire. No one would ever know what became of her unless some unhappy sailor escaped to tell the terrible tale.

At last the men who owned ships in New York grew tired of losing ships and men. They decided to send a brave and honest man named Captain Kidd out to fight pirates and make the sea safe for decent folk. Away sailed Captain Kidd to the coast of Africa, and he fought and captured many a pirate ship.

But the crew of Captain Kidd's boat were a greedy, bold lot. They wished the captain to turn pirate himself and capture friendly ships as well as pirates. One day a sailor named Moore refused to obey him. Captain Kidd in anger picked up a bucket and threw it at Moore. The sailor dropped to the deck. The next day he was dead.

"He mutinied against his captain," said the sea gulls. "He deserved to die."

On sailed Captain Kidd, around Africa and into the Indian Ocean. There he captured a ship that was laden with rich treasure. It carried the wedding gifts for the daughter of the Great Mogul of India. The Great Mogul was furious and he threatened to stop England's trade with India and China.

The people in England became frightened. They did not wish to lose trade with India. Someone must be punished to make peace with the Great Mogul. It must be Captain Kidd's fault.

When Captain Kidd came near home, he heard that people were saying that he had turned pirate. He landed on Gardiner's Island and left his treasure there. When he landed on the main land, the governor arrested him.

Captain Kidd and his friends vowed that he had done no wrong. He had papers to show that he had taken only pirate ships, or ships that belonged to countries at war with England. It did no good. The Great Mogul was angry. Someone must be punished. Besides, the governor himself and even the King of England had been making money secretly in ways that they did not wish known.

Captain Kidd was sent to England to be tried. When the case came to court, the papers that Captain Kidd had brought to show what ships he had attacked, were nowhere to be found. They had disappeared. "Anyway, Captain Kidd killed a man on the voyage," said his enemies. No one listened when Captain Kidd told how Moore had mutinied against him. Captain Kidd was found guilty. He was hanged. His body was left hanging from the gallows.

Years later the papers were found. They showed that what Captain Kidd had said was true. Today some people think that Captain Kidd really *was* a pirate. Others think that he suffered to cover the sins of other men.

AN OLD FIRE ENGINE
First the water was drawn from the well and poured into the engine. Then the men pumped and sent the stream onto the burning house.

(From "Ye Olde Fire Laddies" by Herbert Asbury)

Chapter Sixteen

THE ZENGER TRIAL IN 1735

EACH year New York grew larger. Many changes took place. In 1689 Stuyvesant's wall was pulled down. A famous street shows where it ran. Wall Street it is called, and all the world knows that name.

A new City Hall was built on Wall Street. Two new fire engines were kept in one of its rooms. Men pulled them along the street in case of fire, and worked the pumps by hand, but they were more help than the buckets of Dutch days. One room in the new City Hall was used for the first public library. Another was a prison where people who owed money were kept, until they could pay their debts.

"How are they ever going to pay if they are kept in prison?" wondered the sea gulls, and some people wondered too, so later that law was changed.

Across the street from the City Hall stood the pillory and stocks. Here people who had done wrong were made uncomfortable until they learned better ways. There was a whipping post for greater sinners. But these sights did not drive people away. Many comfortable homes with trees about them lined the street.

There were also places of business on Wall Street. There stood the first refinery to make molasses into white sugar. There was a market where wheat and corn were sold. There was a slave market where whites, Negroes, and Indians were sold or hired out. At the head of Wall Street stood Trinity Church. At the foot, came the ferry from Brooklyn. The fare was twopence for a person, and a shilling for a horse. People used English money now.

At night some streets in New York were lighted. During "the dark of the moon," a lantern was hung from each seventh house. A candle burned in the lantern if the wind or rain did not put it out, or bad boys throw stones at it. The owner of the house upon which the lantern hung, cared for it. The people in the six houses between supplied the candles. So began New York's first street lights.

The old fort still stood on the tip of Manhattan. Some men had rented the ground in front of it for a bowling green, and Bowling Green it is still called to this day. No house has ever been built on that land.

From Bowling Green a stagecoach ran twice a week to Boston. Up Broadway it went with horn blowing to warn

97

EARLY STAGECOACH
Horses were changed at inns along the way and fresh horses were harnessed to the coach. The first set of horses had a chance to rest so that they would be ready for their turn on the return trip.

children, dogs, ducks, and geese to get out of the way. It followed Bowery Lane past Stuyvesant's old farm, to the Boston Post Road. It crossed Spuyten Duyvil Creek by the King's Bridge. The bridge was built near the old "wading place," where men and animals had once forded the shallow water. The king had given permission to have the bridge built so it was named for him, but a toll was charged. This angered the farmers and they built their own bridge that was free to all.

The stagecoach rattled and swayed as it bumped over the rough dirt roads. Some of the men rode on top with the driver, but the ladies preferred to be inside. Everyone had to get out when the heavy coach stuck in a mudhole. The men helped the struggling horses to pull out the heavy coach. Heavy leather straps held the body of the coach instead of springs. Sometimes a strap broke. Sometimes a wheel cracked. Passengers were glad when they reached an inn for the night. But everyone must be up at sunrise the next morning for another day of jolting.

As the years went by, the sea gulls became used to

seeing English governors come and go. Some were good men, some were stupid. Some came rich and went home poor. Some came poor and went home rich. One dressed himself up in woman's clothes and paraded around the fort. One hanged himself after he had been in the city a few days.

There was always excitement when a new governor came. A great feast was served. At one dinner there was served "venison, turkey, chicken, goose, duck and other game, mutton, beef, lamb, pork and sausages with pastry, cakes and choicest wines," so there was no reason for anyone to go hungry.

Governors lately come from London must not find New York dull. So the little city had balls and boating parties on the rivers, horse racing, and, in winter, sleighing. In those days wealthy ladies wore wide hooped skirts of fine silk. Their hair was worn in puffs and curls. Men wore bright-colored coats, red, purple or yellow, over tight short knee breeches; silk stockings and shoes with silver buckles. Lace frills hung from their necks and sleeves. Some wore long curled wigs instead of their own hair.

But life was not all parties and dancing for the governors. The governors quarreled with the men whom the people elected. No money could the governors get unless these men voted taxes. The governor could not even get his own salary, and that was hard for there is not much you can do without money unless you are a sea gull.

One governor had special trouble. His name was Cosby. He was one of the governors who came to New York hoping to grow rich. There were many people who wished to be free of such governors! Two newspapers had been started in the city. One printed only pleasant things about Cosby. The other was against him. It was called the *New*

York Weekly Journal and it was printed by a man named Peter Zenger.

Each week Zenger printed a "Long, loud cry" against what was going on. Cosby was furious. The paper not only criticized him, it made fun of him as well. He decided that Zenger must stop.

But people said, "We want freedom to print the truth. If our governor is good, we will say so. If our governor is greedy and dishonest, we will say so. Truth whether pleasant or unpleasant shall be printed whatever the governor says."

Cosby ordered all copies of the newspaper to be burned by the city hangman. Zenger only printed more. Then Zenger was thrown into prison. His wife kept on printing the paper.

Then Zenger was brought into court to be tried. As many people as could packed into City Hall. Those who could not get inside filled Wall Street. A jury was chosen to hear the case. First the lawyer for the governor spoke. He said that the governor was sent by the king. To criticize the king was treason. Zenger was guilty of treason and should be hanged.

A famous lawyer named Andrew Hamilton had come to defend Zenger. He was old and ill, but he had traveled five days by stagecoach from Philadelphia to see that justice was done. He felt that freedom of speech was a very important thing. People must be able to hear and to speak the truth whether it was pleasing or not to those in power.

Andrew Hamilton rose and spoke to the jury. He said that the people of this country were not willing to be ruled by a governor and to have no right to say whether that governor was just and fair. Zenger had not printed lies.

He could prove that what he had printed was true. Were the people of this country to have no right to say whether a governor was honest or dishonest, whether a law was just or unjust?

When Hamilton finished speaking, the jury decided that Zenger had done no wrong. He had printed the truth. He should go free. The people in the courtroom stood up and cheered and cheered until their shouts could be heard throughout the town and far out on the harbor.

Crowds lined the street as Andrew Hamilton went down to the ferry for New Jersey. He would take no pay for his work, but the city presented him with a gold snuff-box. Two guns at the Battery fired a salute as the old man left.

Freedom to speak and to print the truth is as important today as it was in 1735. In a democracy, people must be able to hear both sides if they are to make up their minds wisely. We must not be afraid to hear the truth whether we like it or not.

It is easier for us to get the news today than it was in Zenger's day. News was slow in traveling. It took two months to get news from England. It took a week for news to come to New York from Boston or Philadelphia. Today telephones and cables, radio and TV bring us the news almost before it happens. Great printing presses work day and night. Over five million papers are bought each day in New York. Two hundred different news-papers are printed in foreign languages so that those who cannot read English may have the news.

The spirit of Peter Zenger is still with us.

Chapter Seventeen

Wars and Stamps

ONE winter the sea gulls saw New York filled to overflowing with soldiers in red uniforms. English soldiers were landing by the thousand.

For many years there had been trouble between the English Colonies in New England and the French Colonies in Canada. There were disputes about land and about the fur trade with the Indians. There had been fighting. Many people had been killed, many lonely farms burned. Now England decided to settle the matter once and for all.

There were not enough barracks in the city for all these soldiers. The governor ordered the people to take them into their homes. The people objected. They said that the governor had no right to force them. The governor became angry. He said the soldiers had come to defend the Americans against the French and Indians. The least the people could do was to give the men a place to sleep. But the people refused.

In the spring the redcoats marched north to Canada.

Some of the American troops went, too. An English general named Braddock was in command. It was hard work marching his men through swamps and dense woodland. The English were not used to fighting in deep woods. The Americans tried to warn them that the French and Indians would be hiding behind trees and would attack suddenly. The English officers would not listen to them.

Suddenly the French and Indians attacked without warning. Shots came from behind trees and rocks. The English marching in line in their red coats were an easy mark. Indian war whoops sounded through the woods.

A young American officer rode among the terrified English soldiers, trying to lead them to attack. Wounded and dead soldiers blocked the trail. Then General Braddock was hit by a bullet. It was the young American who leaped from his horse and held the dying general in his arms. The young soldier's name was George Washington. He was learning a great deal about fighting that was to be useful to him later on.

Other English soldiers pressed on to Canada. The French were defeated. So Canada belonged to England, but to this day many people there speak French. Old French names cling to towns and rivers.

Back to New York went the redcoats to sail for home. But many a lad who had marched bravely out of town had died of wounds or fever in this strange land while his heart longed for English meadows and shady English lanes.

The war was over, but people in this country did not settle down. There were strange happenings in Boston, in New York, and in Philadelphia and Charlestown. People were complaining more and more about the way England was governing her colonies. They did not like English governors like Cosby. They did not like laws that were good for England but bad for this country. Now that the French no longer held Canada, the Americans felt that they did not need English soldiers to protect them. Indeed some people were beginning to feel that they did not need England at all.

"There's sure to be trouble," said the sea gulls, and there was.

It began over stamps. Stamps seem very small things to make so much to-do about, but little things can stand for bigger things. The stamps were a way of taxing the Americans. England needed more money. It had cost a great deal fighting the French and Indians. The English thought that the Americans should pay some of the cost. So they passed a law that said that all important papers like wills and deeds for land, must have stamps put upon them. Each stamp cost money. The money went to England.

"England has no right to tax us without our consent," cried the people. There was talk, talk, talk in kitchens and stores, in fields, at inns, in parlors.

"What is going to happen?" wondered the young gulls.

"We shall see what we shall see," said an old gull, and no one could dispute that.

One October day in 1765 a ship arrived bringing stamps. Flags in the city were put at half mast. Shops were closed. The newspaper was printed with a wide black border. The city was saying: "Our liberty is dead. The king has killed it with this unlawful tax."

Some people wanted to burn the stamps, but the governor had his soldiers carry them to the fort and lock them up. It made some of the people so angry that they stuffed a figure to look like the governor. They stole his coach, put the figure in it, and burned it at Bowling Green.

"What good is that going to do?" wondered the sea gulls, and the calmer people of the city wondered too.

Many of the businessmen of the city met at an inn on Wall Street. They talked the matter over seriously and they solemnly promised to buy nothing that came from England until the hated law was changed. The next ship that came in was laden with salt, coal, and beer. She was sent back to England just as she came.

But just then good news reached New York. The Stamp Act had been changed. No more stamps! The people of New York were so pleased that they ordered a huge statue of King George the Third, who was then the king, to be placed at Bowling Green.

A band of young men who called themselves the Sons of Liberty put up a tall flagpole in The Fields, an open place where our City Hall of today now stands. Some of the English soldiers in the city did not like all these celebrations. They thought the people should obey King George and not make a fuss. They pulled down the flagpole.

The Sons of Liberty put up another with iron bands around it so that it could not be chopped away. For two years the pole stood. But it annoyed the soldiers. They tried to blow it up with gunpowder. At last they got it down and cut it into pieces.

Whenever the Sons of Liberty and the soldiers met there was trouble. One day in January of 1770 there was fighting on Golden Hill. It had been named for its golden fields of wheat, but snow covered the hill that day, and the snow was stained with blood. It was only the beginning.

The new statue of the king arrived. Very grand and

big he looked on a horse. The people were not so sure now that they wanted a statue of King George. Another tax law had been passed in England. The Americans must pay taxes on tea, lead, paper, glass, and paint. The people objected. All the taxes were taken off except the one on tea.

"We'll buy no tea," said the people.

The Sons of Liberty watched the harbor for ships with tea. They sent one back to England. But one captain lied about his cargo. He said he had no tea. The Sons of Liberty found eighteen chests of it hidden. Into the harbor they threw the tea!

The sea gulls tried to eat the little black leaves, but they did not like them. The fish complained bitterly.

In Boston there was still more trouble. One night figures with painted faces and tomahawks climbed aboard a ship. They hacked open tea chests and dumped tea overboard. Then they disappeared mysteriously into the night.

The English governor and the soldiers were furious. Boston was filled with redcoats. Boston harbor was blocked by English warships. Boston must pay for the tea. Boston would not.

Matters were getting so serious that leading men from all the different parts of this country met together. They sent a message to King George asking him to change the law, but nothing came of it. Then the Americans began training soldiers of their own. Men came from far and near. They had no uniforms and many had no guns.

It was a strange little army. Most of the men had never fought. Some stayed only a few weeks and then went back to their farms. They had no idea what it meant to be a soldier. But others worked hard to gather supplies and men. A young American officer was put in charge of

NEW YORK HARBOR IN 1739

Notice the British flag flying over the fort. It was called Fort George at the time that this picture was made.

(From an old print in the New York Public Library)

the army. He had been a young soldier in the French and Indian Wars. His name was George Washington.

There was fighting at Lexington, Concord, and Bunker Hill. Then Washington gathered his men close about Boston. It was no longer a comfortable place for the English. They made ready to leave. Down to the waiting ships they marched.

Where were they going? Back to England? To Canada? Or perhaps by water to New York? Nobody knew and everyone wondered.

Washington and his men came hurrying down from Boston to New York.

Chapter Eighteen

THE DECLARATION OF INDEPENDENCE

WHILE the sea gulls were watching for the English fleet, the men who had met together in Philadelphia were still talking. At first they had no idea of war with England. They only wanted England to make better laws for this country. As time went on, more and more of them began to feel that it would be better if this country separated from England and made its own laws.

Many people, however, did not feel that way.

These people said: "We love England with all our hearts. We speak English. We read English books. Our families and friends are in England. Perhaps England has passed foolish laws, but laws can be changed more easily than hearts."

These people were called Tories. They were loyal to the fine things for which England stood. But, as the days went by, more and more people came to feel that the quarrel between England and her American colonies had gone too far.

"Peace can never be made," they said, "until the two countries are separated."

In July of 1776, the men in Philadelphia drew up a

paper. It was called the Declaration of Independence. It said that the thirteen English colonies in America should separate from England. They should become the United States of America. Horsemen rode out through the land carrying the news. Each year we celebrate the Fourth of July in memory of that famous day.

But the country was not freed from England by just saying so! First there must be fighting. It was a serious matter that had been undertaken.

On the ninth of July, a horseman bearing a copy of the Declaration came galloping into New York City. The soldiers gathered in The Fields. General Washington was there in his blue-and-buff uniform. He looked tall and dignified as he rode his large gray horse.

Solemnly the paper was read aloud. Solemnly the people listened. It was bitter news for the Tories and there were many of them in New York. It was serious news to the men who were fighting. If the war failed, they would be traitors. They would lose their homes and land. If they were caught, they would be hanged. It was a solemn moment for Washington as he looked at the little army before him.

The Sons of Liberty, however, were delighted with the news. They celebrated by pulling down the statue of King George that had so recently been put up. The horse and its rider were made of lead. It was heavy. The men put ropes round it and tugged and pulled. At last the statue came down with a crash.

The pieces were sent to Connecticut. There the women melted them and poured the hot lead into molds to make bullets. Forty thousand bullets were made, so the story goes. There was great need for bullets.

There were more serious things to think about in New

York than pulling down statues. Word had just come that the British fleet had been sighted off Sandy Hook. General Howe and all his men and battleships were at hand. His men had begun landing on Staten Island. The Revolutionary War had reached New York City.

All through the month of August, the sea gulls watched English troops drilling on Staten Island. There were Hessian troops too, who came from Germany. In those day a king often hired soldiers from another country to fight for him.

The British and Hessians had shining uniforms and gleaming guns. The red coats of the British flashed in the sun. Back and forth the soldiers marched on the parade ground. They were splendidly drilled.

On Manhattan, the sea gulls saw far different sights. The American army had no uniforms and few guns. Some of the men were dressed like woodsmen in leather leggings and coonskin caps. They knew a great deal about fighting Indians and hunting, but little about drilling. Other men were dressed like farmers in homespun. What would these men do when the firing began? Would they charge forward together when their officers gave the order?

Washington placed his men where they were most needed around the city. Then he sent all he could spare to fortify Brooklyn. Whoever held Brooklyn Heights would hold the East River and New York City. From Brooklyn Heights, cannon could drop balls into the heart of the city. Washington went back and forth across the East River to see that everything possible was done.

For a month the two armies waited, and the sea gulls waited and wondered what would happen next. Then came the word that boatload after boatload of redcoats was leaving Staten Island and crossing the Narrows to Brooklyn. The men were marching toward the line of wooded hills where the Americans waited. Then the fighting began. The sea gulls screamed and flew away.

There were three roads that led through the hills where the Americans were. Two were well guarded. A patrol of five Americans watched the third as well as they could. One night the British sent a band of scouts along that road, and through the Jamaica Pass, as it was called.

"Halt!" came the cry. "Who goes there?"

But what could five Americans do against a band of British? They were taken prisoners. The way lay open. There was no one left to warn the Americans on the wooded hills beyond.

Down the road in the dark marched the British soldiers. At daybreak the fighting began again. The first thing that the Americans knew the British had surrounded them on three sides. Cannon boomed at them from every direction. Many soldiers were killed or wounded.

Up and down the line rode Washington. He encouraged his men and cheered them on. But the Americans had been badly trapped.

The next days were wet and rainy. At last Washington decided that he must move his men across the East River to join the rest of the army on Manhattan. He must save the men if possible. There was no chance of driving the British back.

Washington sent out his orders. All small boats and barges were to be sent quietly to the Brooklyn shore that night. But what if General Howe should hear of the plan? There were more than four hundred British battleships anchored in the bay.

After dark, the boats gathered silently as Washington

had ordered. Quietly the Americans broke camp. They left their campfires burning. Down the steep cliff to the water they marched. The boats were manned by men from Marblehead in Massachusetts. They were fishermen, and they knew how to handle the work. Swiftly and silently load after load of men were ferried across the dark water.

Some of the men waiting on the shore grew excited and anxious in the darkness. Some pushed and fought for places. Back and forth among the troops rode a dark figure. He spared himself no effort. He encouraged and calmed his men. All night Washington was at his post. All night long the boats went back and forth.

Toward morning a heavy fog settled over the river. The tide was changing and the boats were hard to steer. Then the fog lifted. The sun broke through. The British awoke to discover what was happening. Down the cliff to the shore they came hurrying. The last boatload of Americans was just leaving in safety. The British were too late.

For the next two weeks the American troops stayed in New York City. But there was no hope of holding the city with so many British ships in the harbor and so many British soldiers at hand. Washington moved his headquarters to a house at the north end of Manhattan, overlooking the Harlem River. The lovely old house still stands there for you to visit. It is called the Jumel Mansion.

Orders came for the American soldiers to leave the city. Up to the north end of the island they marched, dragging heavy cannon along dusty roads. It was only just in time.

British warships sailed up the East River. Their guns opened fire on the retreating Americans. Barges of redcoats landed. They attacked the last of the Americans to leave the city.

Some of the Americans became frightened. The sight

of the redcoats so near, the fury of the cannon was too much for them. They were new at fighting. They broke line in confusion. They fled in a panic.

There was a wide cornfield where the New York Public Library now stands at Forty-second Street and Fifth Avenue. Here Washington met these men. He shouted to them to stop their mad flight and behave like soldiers. He struck at them with his sword in anger. It did no good. On went the rush.

Now the British were almost upon them. Washington was too disheartened to care whether he was captured or not. One of his officers caught his horse's rein. The officer turned Washington's horse around quickly, and galloped away with him to safety.

Up the length of Manhattan went the Americans. But not all of them fled in panic. The rest helped save cannon and supplies. The sun beat hot on the fields where now lies Central Park. Across the fields and up the dusty roads hastened the men.

It seemed impossible that all the men could reach safety before the British attacked again. But something lucky happened. The old story goes that General Howe and his officers stopped at the pleasant country place of Mrs. Robert Murray at Murray Hill near where the Grand Central Station stands today. She served them refreshments under cool shady trees. It was pleasant to linger. Every moment gave the Americans more time.

The next morning a party of British sighted some Americans. An English bugler put his horn to his lips. Loud and clear he blew. The call he sounded was the one that hunters use when the fox is sighted. The British had the American fox on the run. The redcoats laughed, but the Americans did not.

Washington chose a band of men that he could trust. He sent them back to attack the British. There was sharp fighting where Barnard College now stands. Back and forth the men charged across a field of buckwheat. The Americans found that they could stand up against the British. They could even drive them back. Courage returned to Washington's troops. By the end of the day, they had proved they were not foxes to be chased for sport.

Some of the American soldiers were sent across the King's Bridge to Westchester. Others crossed the Hudson to Fort Lee on the New Jersey side. Others went to Fort Washington which stood on the high cliff at the north end of Manhattan, not far from where the Cloisters stand today.

THE JUMEL MANSION
Here Washington had his headquarters. The house is still standing.

Chapter Nineteen

THE FALL OF FORT WASHINGTON

FOR several weeks, the Americans waited at Fort Washington, and General Howe waited at the lower end of Manhattan, and the sea gulls waited on the rocks in the East River.

Washington needed badly to know what the enemy was planning to do next. He needed a spy to send into the city. A young officer named Nathan Hale offered to go on the dangerous errand. Spying is risky business. When a spy is caught he is hanged without more ado.

Nathan Hale took off his uniform. He disguised himself as a schoolmaster. Then he journeyed to Long Island. From there he crossed the East River to New York City. He pretended that he had important business in the city and that he had nothing to do with Washington or his army.

Through the streets went Nathan Hale watching all that he could see and listening to all that he could hear. But it was not for long. Someone recognized him. Someone reported to the British that this man was really an officer in the American Army.

Nathan Hale was arrested. He was tried and found guilty of being a spy. The next day he was hanged by the roadside near where Sixty-sixth Street crosses Third Avenue. But he died bravely. His last words were: "My only regret is that I have but one life to give for my country."

It was bitter news for Washington, but he had little time to mourn his young friend. The British and Hessians were closing in on Fort Washington. British battleships were sailing up the Hudson although the Americans had sunk old ships filled with rock to try to block the river.

Other British ships sailed up the East River and landed soldiers on the two islands near Hellgate: Ward's Island and Randall's. Barge after barge full of Hessians came through the Harlem River and landed beneath Fort Washington.

One dark night a man slipped out of the fort. He was an American officer. He was deserting to the British side. Many soldiers had left the American side for they felt that there was no hope of Washington's winning the war. The British were quite used to American deserters. But this man was different. He was an officer. He knew where the guns were stationed in the fort. He knew where the walls were strong and where they were weak. He gave plans of the fort to the British.

The fighting began. One after another the smaller forts around Fort Washington were taken. At one stood a gunner named Corbin, and his wife was with him. She had come to nurse the wounded. Suddenly a shot hit her husband and he fell dead. Margaret Corbin seized the ramrod. She loaded the gun time after time, and fired it in his place. Soon she too fell, but she was only wounded. She was carried across the river to the American camp. Soon she was well and nursing again.

While the fighting was going on, Washington stood on the Palisades. He watched through a field glass. He had been at the fort a short time before, but it was not safe for him to cross the river now, though his heart ached for the men who were fighting. Two hundred years later a huge bridge was to be built across the Hudson at that spot. It is called George Washington Bridge.

Fort Washington was surrounded. There seemed little hope that the men could hold out much longer. Washington sent a last messenger across the Hudson to urge them if possible to hold out until night. Then he would try to rescue them. But the British did not wait. They attacked at once.

At the moment that Washington's messenger arrived, a Hessian general was demanding that the fort surrender. The men inside were given a half hour to talk over what they had best do. There was little good in talking. More and more barges of Red Coats were landing. To fight longer meant death to every man in the fort. There was no escape now.

The messenger was resolved to get back to Washington at all cost. He ran from the fort. He leaped down the steep, rocky cliff to the river amid a rain of bullets. As if by magic he escaped. He jumped into his boat and rowed quickly away.

It was bad news that he had to bring to Washington. The Americans had laid down their arms. Twenty-eight hundred men were taken prisoner. Down the road that is now St. Nicholas Avenue they marched. Tramp, tramp, tramp—they went to prisons in the city.

All Manhattan Island was now in the hands of the British, and there it stayed for seven long years. There was a great fire in the city. Four hundred houses burned. No one troubled to pull down the ruins or build new houses.

The city became a great prison camp for captured American soldiers. The City Hall was turned into a prison. Churches and warehouses were turned into prisons. Ships anchored out in the East River were turned into prisons and miserable men were crowded into them. The sea gulls watched sad sights.

The streets were filled with British officers. Boats kept coming and going filled with troops. The officers amused themselves as well as they could during the seven long winters. They gave balls and put on plays to pass the time. There was horse racing out on Long Island at Jamaica. The son of the King of England came for a visit. He was the first of the royal family to visit this land that it was so soon to lose.

For seven years the fighting went on in other parts of the country. When they met at the nesting places, the sea gulls heard from other gulls news of what had happened. There was a dark night when Washington hurried his men across the Delaware River and surprised the Hessians at Trenton. He captured many.

Other gulls told of a hard winter at Valley Forge. Washington's soldiers had little food and no pay. Many gave up and went home. They were tired of drilling in the snow with no shoes and bleeding feet. But, during the winter, some men came from Europe to help the Americans. There was Lafayette from France and Steuben from Germany. Steuben helped Washington drill his men.

UNIFORMS OF SOLDIERS IN THE REVOLUTION

Under the American flag stands an American soldier. Next him is a French soldier with the French shield above him. Then comes a British soldier under the British flag.

In the spring Washington's army was better trained than it had been at the beginning of that hard winter.

Once during the war, the sea gulls saw Washington again near New York. He was with a French general named Rochambeau. They looked across the Spuyten Duyvil Creek at the forts the English held. They rode through the grounds of Morrisania, the country home of the Morris family on the Harlem River. Lewis Morris had signed the Declaration of Independence for New York. His home was far from a pleasant spot at that time. English cannon balls fell near it from the batteries on Randall's Island where the Triborough Bridge now crosses.

On the heights north of the Harlem River, French troops paraded in fine white broadcloth uniforms with green trimmings. The English watched anxiously to see

what was going to happen. But Washington and Rochambeau decided not to attack the city. Instead, they ordered
their men south.

Then, at last, came the battle of Yorktown. The British
general, Cornwallis, surrendered to Washington. The war
was over. The Americans had won. The United States
was to be a free and independent country. If things went
wrong now, it had no one to blame but itself. The redcoats were to return to England, and very glad they were
to go.

The sea gulls on the East River had almost forgotten
what it was like to have no war. Some of them had been
young gulls with drab, brown feathers when the fighting
began. Now they were old sea gulls with gray wings and
pearly backs and snow-white breasts. They were glad to
have the fighting end.

Chapter Twenty

WASHINGTON'S RETURN

AT LAST came the day when the British soldiers were to leave the city and march down to the shore to sail home to England. The sea gulls flew about the barges and screamed a good-by. People hurried from houses to watch.

Barges filled with redcoats rowed out to the waiting ships. Other people besides soldiers were leaving too. Many Tories were sorry that the United States no longer belonged to England. Their hearts were broken that the war had ended as it had. They were leaving New York to live in some part of the world where the British flag still waved.

Other people in New York were waiting eagerly to welcome the returning American troops and to cheer them as they marched by. Out the Bowery Road these people crowded, past Collect Pond. They met Washington and his soldiers where Union Square is today. A statue of

Washington stands near the spot. The crowd greeted him with joy. They led the way down toward Bowling Green.

Here something unexpected happened. On the high flagpole, the British flag still waved! That was all wrong! Men rushed to pull it down, but it was not so easy to get it down. The British soldiers had greased the pole and pulled off the cleats. As fast as anyone tried to climb the pole, down he slipped! The British thought that they would have time to sail out of the harbor and still see their flag flying over the fort. The Americans felt that something must be done, and done quickly.

Up rushed a man with a hammer and heavy nails. He hammered new cleats to the flagpole. Step by step he climbed, nailing on the cleats as he went. Up and up he went while the people waited breathlessly below. Then came shouts. There was a great boom of guns from the Battery. Down came the British flag. Up went the American.

There waved the American flag for the last of the British soldiers to see. It had thirteen red and white stripes upon it for the thirteen new states. It had thirteen white stars on a blue ground. So, at last, New York became an American city.

Washington did not stay long in New York City. He wished to go back to his peaceful home, Mount Vernon, in Virginia. He longed to be rid of the worries and cares that he had carried for seven long years of war. He had come to the city to say good-by to his soldiers and his officers. He had come to urge them to work with all their hearts to make this country a happy one in which to live.

It was at Fraunces Tavern, which still stands at the corner of Pearl and Broad streets amid the hurry and bustle of our big city, where Washington said farewell to

THIRTEEN STRIPES AND THIRTEEN STARS

his officers. All were glad that the fighting was over. Nevertheless the parting was hard. They had all worked together. They had suffered together. They had shared hopes and black fears. Now they were to go home to make the new country a success in peace as well as in war. That is sometimes harder to do than fight.

Washington spoke to the men. "With a heart full of love and gratitude, I now take leave of you," he said gravely. "I most devotedly wish that your latter days may be as prosperous and happy as your former ones have been gracious and honorable."

One by one the officers came up and shook his hand. Many had tears rolling down their faces. Then Washington turned and left the room.

At Whitehall Ferry, near the Battery, a barge waited to carry him on the first part of his journey to Mount Vernon. People lined the streets. They stood silently as he passed among them. As he stepped into the barge, a loud cheer rang out. Washington waved his hat. The boat swung out into the river.

Then Washington looked back at the old fort. Here the Indians had come to talk to Kieft and to sit in solemn council smoking the peace pipe. Here Stuyvesant had stamped in fury when his men refused to fight. Here English governors had come and English governors had gone. But no Dutch or English governors would come to these shores again.

How should New York be governed? Three men named John Jay, Robert Livingston, and Gouverneur Morris had been busy making laws for the state of New York. George Clinton had been elected the first governor. James Duane was the new mayor of the city. But there was more than the city and state to plan for. How was the new United States of America to be governed? That was a very big question.

"Won't there be trouble and disputing over getting everything settled in a new way?" wondered the sea gulls.

There certainly was trouble. One state wanted things done one way. Other states wanted things done other ways. For six years there was little else besides disputing. The country that Washington and his men had fought for nearly fell to pieces. Some people felt that each one of the thirteen states should be free to pass whatever laws it wished. Other people felt that this country would never be strong unless the states could work closely together.

At last a paper was drawn up. It was called the Federal Constitution. The Constitution said that the country as a whole should elect a president. Each state should send men to congress to meet together to vote on laws for the country as a whole, but each state might settle its own home affairs as it wished. When the good of the whole country was concerned, then the president and congress should have the power to say how things should be.

Some people were all for the Constitution. Other people were against it. They said the Constitution protected rich people rather than poor people. They said that a president and a congress which could make them do what they did not want to do, would be as bad as a king. They had just fought a war to get rid of a king. These people carried a copy of the Constitution down to Bowling Green and burned it.

As time went on, however, more and more of the thirteen states agreed to the Constitution and signed it. In New York City, the people who were for the Constitution held a great procession. The sea gulls were very much interested in it. Five thousand people marched. The bakers baked a loaf of bread that took a whole barrel of flour and marched with it on a float. The hatters and the men who made wigs had their float, and the workers in leather who made all the shoes and gloves by hand. The iron-workers and the carpenters, the upholsterers and the furriers, and all the tradesmen of the city marched.

Then came a boat on wheels. It was drawn by horses. The sea gulls were much interested. They had never seen a boat on land before. But when it reached the fort, the thirteen guns on this boat fired a salute to the thirteen states. The sea gulls left hurriedly.

The ship was called the *Federal Ship Hamilton,* for a man named Alexander Hamilton was working as hard as he could to get people to agree to the new Constitution. And many men all over the state were beginning to feel as he did. They felt that some other nation would conquer the land for which they had fought, unless the thirteen states could stand together.

Three days later, the guns on the fort boomed again. This time it was because the state of New York had accepted the Constitution. So many states had now signed it, that it became the law of the land.

So now the country was to have a president. There was no doubt in anyone's mind as to who that president would be. It must be George Washington.

So back to New York came Washington. He was greeted with music and flowers and processions all the way from Mount Vernon to New York City where he was to live. The sea gulls flew about his head as he landed at Coffee House Slip at the foot of Wall Street.

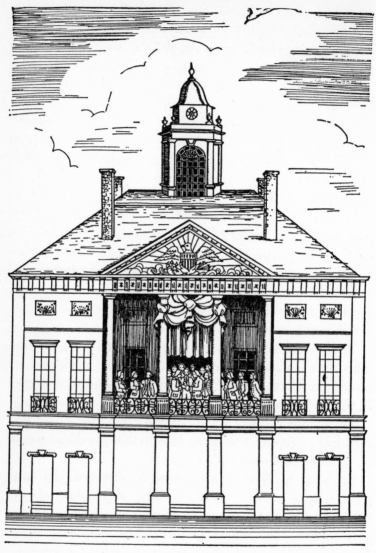

WASHINGTON BEING MADE PRESIDENT AT FEDERAL HALL
ON WALL STREET
(From the Iconography of Manhattan Island, by I. N. Phelps Stokes)

Chapter Twenty-one

THE FIRST PRESIDENT

ON THE 30th of April in 1789 George Washington
became the first President of the United States. He
stood on the balcony of City Hall on Wall Street. It had
been made over for the occasion and was now called Federal Hall, but the sea gulls knew it was really the same
building. The streets, the windows of the houses nearby,
and the roofs were crowded with people. Everyone wished
to see the great sight.

Washington was dressed in a brown homespun suit.
He would wear no fine clothes that had to be bought
from England. His hair was powdered and tied at the
back of his head as men wore their hair in those days.
At his side hung his sword with a plain steel hilt. Straight
and tall he stood, well over six feet in height.

Washington laid his right hand on the Bible. He swore
to serve his country faithfully. He promised to do his best

to live up to the trust the people had placed in him. It was a solemn moment.

Then Chancellor Livingston, who stood in front of Washington, turned to the people in the street below and said, "Long live George Washington, President of the United States."

At the same instant a flag was raised on the building. It was the signal for the guns at the Battery to thunder forth a salute to the new President. Shouts and cheers burst from the people on every side. One man who watched that day wrote, "Such thundering peals went up from the crowds as seemed to shake the foundations of the city, and long and loud were they repeated as if their echoes would never cease."

Washington had driven to Federal Hall in a coach and four. He left in on foot and walked among the crowds to St. Paul's Chapel on Broadway. There a service was held and there today you can see the pew where he sat and prayed for help to meet the problems that he knew lay ahead.

That night, there was a celebration. Processions marched through the streets and there was a great display of fireworks. The sea gulls got little sleep.

Today a bronze statue of Washington marks the place where he was made President. It stands on the broad granite stairway of a new Federal Hall on Wall Street. The slab of brown sandstone from the balcony of the old Federal Hall upon which he stood is saved under glass.

For the next few years President Washington lived in New York with Mrs. Washington and her two grandchildren. A house had been made ready for the President on Cherry Street. It was a big, square, red brick house, four stories high, with many windows and doors. It was one of the most comfortable houses in the city, and it was well furnished with handsome rugs and furniture, fine china and silver. There was a stable with room for many horses and coaches. Today one of the piers of Brooklyn Bridge covers the spot where that house stood.

Often the President and his wife and the grandchildren drove in their coach about the city. The streets of the town were well shaded and pretty. White stone steps led up to many of the brick houses. The blinds at the windows were painted green, and the doorknobs and knockers were of shining brass.

One day the sea gulls saw the President walking down Broadway with a strange group around him. Down the street he came with several Indian chiefs dressed in fine deerskin decorated with porcupine quill and beads. Their faces were gayly painted. They wore great headdresses of feathers.

They were Indians who lived far to the south of New York. The white people were taking more and more of their land for farms. In the backwoods there was fighting going on. Washington had sent for twenty-nine powerful chiefs to come to New York to try to make peace, and to show the warriors the wonders of the city.

The Indian visitors were received by white men dressed as Indians. There was a society in the city that had been formed to foster love for this new land in the hearts of the people. It was named for a famous Indian warrior, Tammany. At the meetings of the society, the members wore Indian costumes. So here were the members of Tammany dressed in war paint and feathers to receive the real Indians.

Dinners and receptions were given for the red warriors. Then a treaty of peace was signed with them. Washington gave the Indians presents. The braves danced and sang for him. They called him "Washington, the Great Sachem of the Thirteen Fires." Then back to their homes in the forests went the Indians. The members of Tammany washed off the war paint and changed their clothes, and went back to their offices and stores and warehouses.

Every year brought changes in the city. In 1790 the old fort at last was pulled down. The sea gulls were really sorry to see it go. A fine new house was built in its place. The Government House it was called. It was intended for the President, but Washington never lived there. The Governor of the state of New York lived there instead.

For a few years, there were many important people living in New York. The President of the United States lived there. The Governor of New York State lived there, and also the Mayor of the city of New York. Congress met in New York. But it was not for long.

First the people of Philadelphia wanted the President to live in their city. Then Congress decided to build an entirely new city for the capital of this country. So the city of Washington was laid out on the banks of the Potomac River.

Soon the governor moved to Albany, so now we have only the mayor of the city living in New York. In front of the mayor's house, a lantern always hangs to show the people where to find him in case of need. First it was a lantern with a candle burning inside. Then it was an oil lamp. Then it was gas, and now it is an electric light.

The mayor lives now in the beautiful old Gracie Mansion that was built in 1799. It stands at Eighty-ninth Street and the East River in Carl Schurz Park, and it looks out over Hellgate where once Adrian Block sailed *The Restless.*

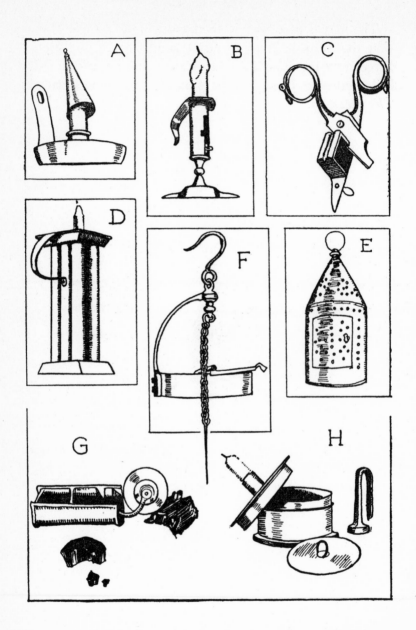

HOW HOUSES WERE LIGHTED AND FIRE MADE

A and B—Two Kinds of Candle Sticks. The first one has a pointed cap which was used to put out the flame.

C—Candle Snuffer. This was used to trim the wick when the flame did not burn evenly.

D—Candle Molds. Candle wicks were placed in the molds and melted wax or tallow was poured around them. The tallow was made from meat fats, especially mutton fat. The wax was from beeswax. Wax candles were better than tallow candles, but they were much harder to get. Tallow candles had an unpleasant smell and were likely to smoke.

E—A Lantern. A candle burned inside the lantern which protected the flame from the wind.

F—A Whale Oil Lamp. The little dish was filled with oil and a wick laid in it. One end of the wick was in the oil. The other was lighted. The little poker was used to adjust the wick.

G—A Steel Wheel and Flint. To make fire, a string was wound around the wheel and it was spun rapidly against the flint. Sparks flew and were caught in a tinder box.

H—A Tinder Box. Tinder was old, scorched linen, which caught fire easily. When the tinder blazed up, a splinter of wood was lighted for a match. It was slow work getting a fire started!

WATER PEDDLER

Water from the Tea Water Pump was sold through the streets. It was much the best water to be had in the town. Most of the wells gave such poor water that even horses refused it.

Chapter Twenty-two

NEW YORK IN WASHINGTON'S DAY

IN MANY ways the New York of Washington's day would seem a strange place to sea gulls of today. Many thousands of pigs still wallowed in the streets, and ate up the garbage that was thrown out to them. Now and again cows strayed down the street. Carts rattled past. Loads of firewood were dumped in front of the houses. Out on the sidewalks, Negro slaves cut the wood with saws into the right lengths for the fireplaces.

There was little or no running water. Into a few kitchens the water was piped through wooden pipes, but not into many. Most of the water was carried from wells that

THE TEA WATER PUMP AT CHATHAM STREET

stood at the street crossings at every fourth block. Into the houses in buckets, the water must be carried, and out again in buckets to be dumped into the gutter or carried to the nearest river.

The water was very poor except that which came from the Tea Water Pump at Chatham Street. The Tea Water Spring gave excellent water. And however much water was taken out, there was always three feet of water left, no more, no less. Carts came all day long to fill their casks at the pump, and to peddle water through the streets.

Many other things were sold through the streets too. Up and down went the tradespeople calling their wares:

Here's clams, here's clams, here's clams today.
They lately came from Rockaway.

137

> They're good to roast, they're good to fry,
> They're good to make a clam potpie.
> Here they go.

People who wished clams for dinner must hurry out to catch the clam-man as he went by.

The milkman carried a yoke on his shoulders from which hung two cans of milk. He called out loudly so that all the world might hear. In the afternoon, there would come the good smell of hot gingerbread and hot muffins, cooked fruit and vegetables for sale.

> Baked pears, baked pears, fresh baked, baked pears!
> Hot corn, hot corn, here's your lily hot corn!

Then a wagonload of sand would come by, fresh white sand to sprinkle on your kitchen floor.

> Here's your white sand; choice sand.
> Here's your lily white s-a-n-d.
> Here's your Rock-a-way beach
> S-a-n-d.

Cattails for poor people, who could not afford feather-beds, to use in mattresses; yeast to raise fresh bread; straw, potatoes, rags, each had its call. So all day long it went. Now and again a butcher would come by leading a fine fat cow or sheep. He would stop at the houses of his customers to take orders for the best cuts of meat.

The first call of all came early in the morning. The children would hear:

> Sweep o-o-o
> From the bottom to the top
> Without rope or ladder
> Sweep o-o-o.

Inside the houses, there were no furnaces. Kitchen stoves had not yet been invented. There were no warm

KITCHEN IN THE OLD DAYS

Notice the woman who is churning cream into butter in her wooden churn, the woman spinning flax, and the woman cooking over the open fire. See the Dutch oven to the left of the fireplace, and the broom made of twigs. Dried herbs hang from the rafters. The grandfather clock stands in the corner. The plates are neatly set in the rack.

(From an old print in the New York Public Library)

bathrooms. In winter, bedrooms were icy places. Children would race downstairs to dress in front of the great kitchen fireplace where breakfast was cooking over the open fire.

There were no refrigerators. Ice was very hard to get. Food must be carried down into the cellar to be kept cool.

George Washington never saw a match. Fire was still made with flint and steel. A string was wound around a wheel made of steel. A quick pull on the string made the wheel spin. The flint was held against the wheel. Sparks flew. The sparks were caught on a bit of old burned rag, or tinder as it was called. From the blazing rag, a stick with sulphur on it was lighted, and the flame carried to the fireplace, or to father's pipe, or to the whale oil lamp, or to the hand-dipped candle.

There were no latchkeys in the city. House keys were six to eight inches long. There were no doorbells. Big brass knockers hung on the doors. Rat-a-tat-tat they sounded when visitors came. There were no house numbers. Shops hung out signs with pictures on them. *Two Running Horses* was the name of a livery stable, and its sign showed two galloping steeds. The tinsmith shop was *The Cat and the Kettle,* and on its sign a comfortable tabby slept in front of a tin kettle. *The Sun and Breeches* was a tailor's shop. People often told where they lived by the nearest shop sign.

"We live three doors south of *The Whistling Pig,*" they would say.

The first sidewalks were laid in New York City in 1790. They were of bricks and very narrow. Two people could hardly pass each other.

There were no sewing machines in Washington's day.

All the men's shirts and suits, all the ladies' full skirts, all the children's clothes had to be sewed by hand. Most of the cloth was still made of homespun thread and woven on looms at home. There were no washing machines. Soiled clothes were taken to a stream if one was near at hand. If not, water for washing clothes was heated in a big iron kettle and poured into wooden tubs.

At school, the boys and girls sat on stiff wooden benches. They learned their letters from hornbooks. They learned to read from the New England Primer and Webster's Spelling Book. School was long and dull. Spelling matches were the only fun. But children in those days were expected to work hard, especially the boys, for there was a college for them to go to in New York now. It had been called King's College before the war. Now it was called Columbia. Washington brought his stepson to study there.

Another young man who came to New York to study was Alexander Hamilton. Later he was an officer in the Revolution. Then he worked to have the Constitution adopted. He started New York's first bank. Hamilton lived on Washington Heights, in a charming house called The Grange. It still stands. There he lived with his wife and seven children.

There was one custom in those days that the sea gulls never could understand. This is the sort of thing that happened now and again. Early one summer's day, a few years after Washington had left New York, the gulls saw two boats cross the Hudson to the Jersey shore. Several men landed at Weehawken and climbed the steep rocky cliff. At the top was a level spot hidden in the woods.

Two of the men held pistols. They walked a little apart. At a signal, they were to turn and fire at each other. It was all because these two men had quarreled.

"I don't see how this is going to settle anything," wondered an old sea gull.

It was the custom in those days. A man was considered a coward if he was asked to fight and did not. This was a duel, and the two men who held pistols were Alexander Hamilton and Aaron Burr. Burr was the Vice President of the United States at that time. But Burr and Hamilton felt very differently on many subjects. Finally Burr became angry at Hamilton. He challenged him to fight a duel.

So the two men stood on the cliff at Weehawken. The signal was given. The men raised their pistols. Hamilton did not fire. Burr did. Hamilton dropped to the ground. His friends rushed to him. He was carried to the boat and rowed across the river. He died the next day.

When people heard what had happened, they were furious. Burr fled secretly from his home. But one good thing came of the duel. More and more people were feeling that duels were a foolish way of settling quarrels. As they talked about the Hamilton-Burr duel, these people felt more strongly than ever that this sort of thing must stop. Hamilton's oldest son had been killed in a duel three years before, on the same spot where his father fell. Duels were stupid and cruel. Civilized men should settle their quarrels in other ways.

So strongly did people feel that the time was soon to come when there would be no more duels on the Jersey shore.

"And a good thing it is," said the sea gulls.

THE "CLERMONT"
(From an old print)

Chapter Twenty-three

MONSTER BREATHING SMOKE AND FLAME

FOR some time the sea gulls watched a strange ship being built at Corlear's Hook on the East River. It was awkward and ugly. It had two big wheels, one on each side. It had a high, black smokestack.

When it was finished, it went chug-chugging round the end of Manhattan and over to the Jersey shore. Black smoke poured from the smokestack. The wheels turned round and pushed the boat through the water. The sea gulls were very much amazed. They flapped their gray wings and screamed to each other.

Robert Fulton had invented a steamboat. For some time, many men in Europe and America had been experimenting with steam engines. They wanted to make water and fire and steam work for them. In England, several engines were being used to pump water and to pull funny little trains of coal cars in the mines. Men were beginning to feel that engines might be very useful friends of man. Now Fulton was making an engine run his boat for him.

"What a strange idea!" cried the young sea gulls.

Other men had tried it before. John Fitch had made a small steamboat that had run round and round Collect Point, but it was only a toy. He had done nothing with the idea and the little boat had finally rotted away.

In 1807, Fulton finished his boat and he named it the *Clermont*. He said that he would run it on a trial trip up the Hudson to Albany. Many people laughed at him. They called the boat Fulton's Folly. They said that the boiler would burst and that Fulton would be blown to bits for his trouble.

Fulton invited several men to go on this first trip. They were none of them eager to accept, but they did not like to show that they were afraid. They stood on deck "sad, silent, and weary." A crowd gathered to see the start.

The fire under the boiler of the *Clermont* was well-stoked with pine wood. A cloud of smoke rose from the smokestack. The big wheels began to churn up the water. Out started the *Clermont* bravely on her way. But she did not go far. Soon her wheels stopped turning. She floated helplessly on the water.

"Dear, dear," cried the sea gulls.

A great many people began to say, "We told you so."

But Fulton asked for half an hour to repair his engine. Suddenly the wheels began to turn again. This time they did not stop.

Up the Hudson River went the *Clermont*. Up the same river where Indian braves had paddled their dugout canoes. Up the same river where the *Half Moon* had sailed, steamed the little *Clermont*. She paid no attention to wind and tide. It made little difference to her which way the wind blew, and which way the current flowed. For the first time in history, ships were free from wind and tide.

As the *Clermont* steamed past, people on shore gazed in wonder. Sparks flew from the smokestack of the little boat, and after dark she looked as though she were on fire. "A great sea monster breathing smoke and flame," people called her. Up to Albany puffed the monster, and back to New York in half the time it took a sailboat.

People soon became used to steamboats. In a few years Fulton had steam ferries running between Manhattan and New Jersey, and one to Brooklyn.

Fulton tried other kinds of boats. He made a submarine, or "diving boat" as he called it. He made a torpedo that could blow up a ship. One day he fired his torpedo at an old empty ship near Governors Island. The ship was blown to bits. The sea gulls flew away as fast as they could go.

Fulton hoped that his inventions would stop wars. If ships could be blown up so easily, there would be no reason for sea battles. Little did he know the sights that later sea gulls were to look upon!

Other matters besides steamboats and torpedoes were being talked about in New York in Fulton's day. The city was growing so large that a group of men was appointed to plan new streets. The whole of the Island of Manhat-

PIG ON THE STREETS OF NEW YORK
(From an old children's book making fun of the condition of
New York streets)

tan was laid out on paper, although only a beginning was made in actually laying out blocks.

The men decided that the new streets should all run straight. Avenue should run north and south. The ones farthest east were to have letter for names, Avenue A, Avenue B, Avenue C, and Avenue D. Then came twelve avenues with numbers for names. Streets crossed the avenues, running east and west, and they too were numbered. Unfortunately these men laid out the avenues far apart. They thought that people would use the rivers to get up and down town. Little did they imagine the cars and busses and trucks that would crowd our streets today.

The new plan did not change the old streets downtown. They were left with their old names. They twisted and turned as the old narrow lanes and cowpaths had done, and so they do today. But uptown the new streets run in straight and orderly lines except for Broadway which cuts across streets and pays no attention to city planners.

It was once an animal trail along the top of a ridge. Then Indians used it. Then the Dutch used it. It is the oldest street in the city, and one of the longest in the world for it runs a hundred and forty seven miles to Albany.

Many people objected to the new streets. Sometimes a street ran through a garden or even a house. One was planned to go right through an old lady's kitchen. It made no difference. All avenues must run straight north and south. All streets must run straight east and west.

"Rather stupid," said the sea gulls.

Hills were leveled to make streets even. The brook that wandered through the swamp between Collect Pond and the Hudson was made to run underground in the narrow walls of a sewer. A road was laid out above it called Canal Street.

Finally Collect Pond itself was filled in. Once it had been lovely with clear water and green banks. But ill-smelling tanneries had been put up along its shores. The water from the pond was used to soak hides. Rubbish had been thrown into it. It was dirty and ugly.

Some people suggested that the land be cleared around it for a park, and the water kept pure. But, no, Collect Pond must be filled in to make more room for streets and buildings. A prison was built on the spot where the Dutch had skated in winter and boated in summer. It was called The Tombs, and to this day a prison stands near that spot.

"Perhaps," say the sea gulls, "if New York had more open green places for fresh air and fun, it would have fewer people who had to be put in prison."

But gulls are only birds, and what do they know about the needs of men?

BROADWAY AND CITY HALL IN 1819
City Hall still stands but high buildings tower above it.
(From the Iconography of Manhattan Island, by I. N. Phelps Stokes)

A new city hall was built. It was the biggest and finest
building in the country. The stone was brought by oxcart
from New England. The farmers along the way complained that the loads were so heavy that they broke
down their bridges. City Hall still stands. It is no longer
the biggest building in the city, but it is one of the most
beautiful and that is far more important. Inside, the lovely
staircase divides and curves in a circle to the upper floor.
The rooms where the mayor of the city and the council
work are decorated with panels of fine wood and with
delicate carvings. On the walls hang portraits of men
who have helped make our city great. City Hall Park
was once The Fields where stood the Liberty Pole, and
where the Declaration of Independence was read. Today
a Liberty Pole and a statue of Nathan Hale stand in the
park.

The year 1812, when City Hall was just finished, saw
many soldiers in New York City. The United States and
England were at war again. American soldiers hurried to
the city, to be ready in case of attack. English warships
were threatening New York Harbor. Forts were being
made ready. Shops and schools were closed. Everyone
worked shoveling dirt. Children who were too small to
hold shovels carried dirt on shingles.

Then word came that the English had captured the
new city of Washington. They had burned the buildings.
In New York, everyone worked harder than ever. But no
attack was made. After two years the war ended. When
peace was made there was a fine display of fireworks
from the new city hall. Every house in New York was
illuminated. Everyone gave a great sigh of relief.

All night the sky was filled with skyrockets. The sea

gulls would think that the sun was rising, and it was time to get up. But just as they started to stretch their wings, the rocket would fade away and it would be night again.

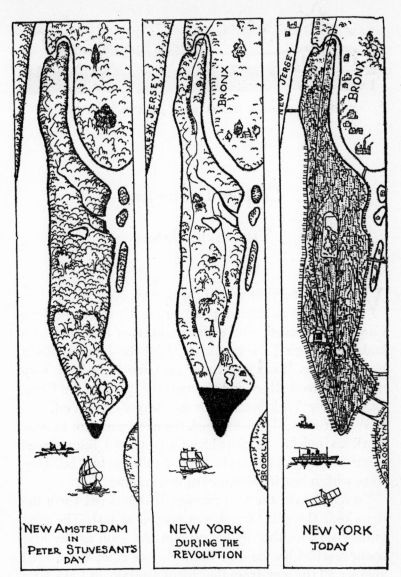

MAPS OF MANHATTAN ISLAND

The first map shows how much of Manhattan was covered by the Dutch town. The second shows how much was covered by the English town. The last one shows how much is covered by the American town of today. Notice how long and thin Manhattan Island is.

HORSES PULLING A CANAL BOAT ON THE ERIE CANAL

Chapter Twenty-four

THE ERIE CANAL

WHEN the War of 1812 was over, New York Harbor became a busy place again. In 1825, the Erie Canal was opened. For eight years, two thousand men had been digging the canal. It joined the Hudson River to Lake Erie. Boats could now go from New York City up the Hudson River and through the canal to the Great Lakes. New York became the gateway to the West.

When the canal was finished, the news was sent to New York as quickly as possible. Cannon had been placed along the way. They were several miles apart, but they were within hearing distance of one another.

"BOOM!" went the first cannon. It thundered forth the news that the great canal was opened at last. The next gunner was waiting by his cannon. As soon as the first boom reached his ears, he fired. So one cannon followed another all the way from the city of Buffalo on Lake Erie to New York three hundred and sixty-two miles away. It took one hour and thirty minutes.

Then a procession of gaily decorated boats started

through the canal. Horses walked along the towpath by the side of the canal and pulled the barges. Four beautiful gray horses pulled the barge in which the Governor of the State sat. His name was De Witt Clinton. He had worked for many years to raise money to build the canal, and to plan where it should go and how it should be made.

Other barges followed. One was called *Noah's Ark*. On it were two of each kind of animal that was found in the forests of our great country. There were two bears, two deer, two foxes, two porcupines rattling their quills, two beavers grawing at trees. There were many other kinds of animals, and there were two slim Indian boys in deerskin to care for them. They were kept busy.

When the procession of barges reached New York, twenty-nine steamships and a large flock of sea gulls went out to meet it. Whistles blew. Bells rang. Flags waved. Out to sea went the boats. Then Governor Clinton raised a cask of water. The water was from Lake Erie. Solemnly he poured it into the ocean to show that the waters of Lake Erie now ran into New York Bay.

When the Governor landed, there was a procession five miles long to greet him. The night sky was filled with fireworks. City Hall was lighted with two thousand candles and lamps.

In a few days the celebrations were over, but the barges did not stop going back and forth through the canal. The boats were pulled by mules and their drivers walked beside them. They sang:

> I've got a mule and her name is Sal,
> Fifteen miles on the Erie Canal!

Loads of furs, lumber, corn, wheat, beef, wool, iron and coal came from the West to be sold in New York.

Then back went the barges carrying passengers and the hundred and one things that pioneers need: cloth, tools, wagons, and supplies.

Before the canal was built it had cost a hundred dollars to carry a ton of goods from New York to Buffalo. Now it cost only six dollars a ton. More and more trade came to New York City because of the canal. The city grew larger. Within a year of the opening of the canal, five hundred new places of business were started. There were twelve new banks and thirteen new insurance companies. With the opening of the Erie Canal New York fast became a more important port than Boston or Philadelphia. Soon it was the most important port in the United States, .and so it is today.

Down along the water front the streets were crowded with trucks. Barrels, sacks, boxes, and hogsheads were piled high on the wharves. The ships were crowded along South Street. Their bowsprits reached almost across the street and into the windows of the houses opposite. Their masts looked like a forest of bare trees with a tangle of ropes and rigging.

Some of the ships were the beautiful, swift clipper ships that were built for the China trade. They carried mountains of white sails as they sped down the harbor, and they seemed to fly over the water. There was no Panama Canal in those days. Ships had to sail around the southern tip of South America to get to the Pacific Ocean. It was a long, dangerous trip.

Each year the clipper ships raced each other to see which could bring in the new crop of China tea first. Their captains were proud of their ships. They gave them names like Flying Cloud, Snow Squall, Lightning and

THE "FLYING CLOUD" A FAMOUS CLIPPER SHIP

Comet. The sea gulls loved to see the clipper ships sail into port.

But the days of clipper ships did not last long. Each year there were more steamships chugging around the harbor. They looked very ugly beside the clipper ships, but they had come to stay. In 1819 the *Savannah* crossed the Atlantic Ocean in twenty-six days. Then the *Great Western* made the trip in fifteen days. All the first steamers had sails as well as engines.

At first, people were very nervous about these engines. Boilers blew up and engines broke down. But better and better engines were made. People began to find them surer and safer. Regular steamship trips between New York and England started.

Down in the hot depths of the steamers, men shoveled coal into the furnaces. Day and night, they must work to keep the hungry fires blazing. Passengers on deck in the fresh air forgot about the stokers down in the engine room.

"We'd rather be sailor lads than stokers," said the sea gulls. "We'd rather climb the masts even in wind and snow, rather than stay down in those hot, stuffy places."

But no one asked the sea gulls' opinion upon the matter. Steamers had come, and come to stay. New York Harbor grew busier each year.

THE ERIE CANAL TODAY

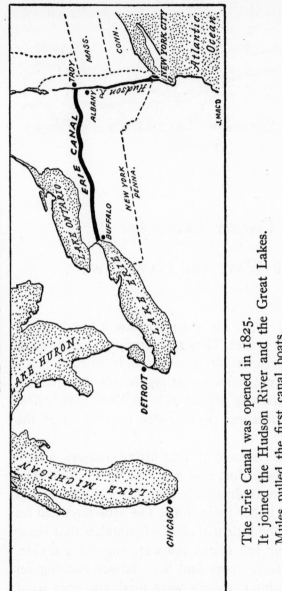

The Erie Canal was opened in 1825.
It joined the Hudson River and the Great Lakes.
Mules pulled the first canal boats.
Today the canal boats have diesel engines.
Locks raise the boats so that they can go up hill.
The highest lock raises them forty feet.
Today boats can go 1,400 miles inland from New York.
It takes five days from Detroit to New York by water.
It takes eight days from New York to Chicago.
Today, New York State canals carry over 5,000,000 tons of freight a year.

SLEIGHING

Chapter Twenty-five

NEW WAYS AND NEW LAWS

ONE day in 1831, the sea gulls saw a great crowd gathered together. They saw strange shining tracks laid along the ground and coaches ready to run on the tracks. There were horses waiting to pull the coaches. The mayor of the city was to ride in New York's first railway. Indeed this was the first street railway in all the world.

The mayor was dressed in tight-fitting trousers, a high hat made of beaver fur, and a frilled white shirt. The ladies with him were dressed in high-waisted dresses and big bonnets tied under their chins. The little boys had on tight suits, and the little girls had on pantalets that hung down under their full skirts. All were eager for a ride.

For several years there had been busses running on Broadway. In winter, sleighs were used, and they went dashing along with a great jingling of bells. But this was the first coach to run upon a track. Away went the four horses. The coach seemed to fly along, so easily and smoothly it ran.

The horse railway was called New York and Harlem Line. At first the tracks ran on Fourth Avenue only as far as Sun Fish Pond at Thirty-third Street. Later they went up to Forty-second Street. It took five years to lay the track all the way to Harlem. It was a big piece of work. At Murray Hill and at Yorkville, deep cuts and tunnels had to be blasted through hard granite rock. Fourth Avenue was the hilliest and rockiest of all the avenues. That was why the city gave the railway permission to use it. No one else wanted to.

At last the track to Harlem was finished. People quite enjoyed the ride. It was country most of the way, with pigs and goats running loose. Then came an exciting day. An engine instead of horses was to pull the coaches. Again people gathered to see the great sight. Some people thought that the smoky, dirty engine would ruin the city. The sea gulls rather agreed with them as they flew above the town to watch the strange sight.

There were few engines in the United States at that time. A New York man, named Peter Cooper, had built the first one. It was called The Tom Thumb because it was so small. But small as it was, it proved that it could be useful. Now New York was to have an engine to pull its street railway.

Suddenly one day the engine blew up in the Yorkville Cut. There was a great boom and a bang—the boiler of the engine had burst. People were badly frightened. Some were hurt. The engine was ruined, so horses had to be used again.

THE "DE WITT
The first railway carriages were just like old

"It's quite as well," said many people as they shook their heads over these new inventions.

Another engine was ordered for the road. It blew up at Fourteenth Street. Several people were killed.

"It is dreadful!" screamed the sea gulls. "Why don't people learn to fly as we do, and be done with iron and steam?"

Still a third engine was ordered. Down the track it ran.

"Look out! Look out!" screamed the gulls.

At what is Fifty-eighth Street and Park Avenue today, was a herd of cows. They wandered across the track in front of the train. The engineer slammed on his brake, but it was too late.

"This is too much!" said many people. "Even cows are no longer safe in New York."

But steam engines had come to stay on land, just as they had come to stay on water. They pulled passengers and they pulled freight. Gradually they became safer and surer. There were fewer and fewer accidents. But many people still complained of the dirt and noise. The city

CLINTON" AND TRAIN
stage coaches except that they ran on tracks.

passed a law that steam engines could only go to Fourteenth Street. But the main station was down near City
Hall. What was to be done? The engines had to stop at
Fourteenth Street. So strong, patient horses were fastened to the coaches and drew them the last part of the
way.

Then the city passed another ruling. No engines below
Twenty-sixth Street. New York did not like the smoke,
dirt, and noise. Horses had still farther to pull the coaches.
But that was not all. The next rule was no engines below
Forty-second Street.

Forty-second Street seemed way out in the country in
those days, but there the trains had to stop, and there they
stop to this day. The Grand Central Station stands there
now. Room for tracks and platforms have been blasted
out of the rock beneath it. There is a whole city there
underground. The tracks leading to the station have been
lowered and covered and the street above them is called
Park Avenue. High buildings tower above it. But no one
knew that that was going to happen in 1831.

No one knew how important railways were to be in making New York the important center that it is today. Another line, The Hudson River Line, was built along that river. Passengers and freight could be carried to Albany far faster than by the river boats. The boat owners were furious, but there was nothing they could do about it.

Even in 1831, the city was growing so large that it took too long to walk from one part to another. Busses and steam cars and street railways were needed, and many people rode on them. Other things were needed too.

More people meant more children, and more children meant more schools. In 1806, a society had been started to build free schools so that every child might have an education. It was the beginning of New York City's great public schools.

"Any child in this city that wants an education has a chance," said a young sea gull.

"If he's got the wits to use it," added an old black-backed gull who had been around a good deal.

The gulls prefer sunlight and blue water and fresh air themselves, but gulls don't have to get on in the world. They just stay as they are born, and make the best of it.

Other big changes came in the city. All Negro slaves were freed in New York State. There had been many Negroes in New York City ever since Dutch days. Negroes had done much for New York. Many were already free. People were feeling, more and more, that slavery was a great wrong. Now there were to be no more slaves in New York.

Another law was passed which said that all men who lived in New York were allowed to vote. Before that, only those men who owned property could vote. It was not until many years later that women were given the vote. Another new law said that the city should vote for its own mayor. Before that the governor of the state had appointed him. Now the people could choose their own.

In the years to come, New York was to have good mayors and bad mayors. Whatever kind they get, the people have only themselves to thank or blame. A good mayor means a healthy, clean, safe city, with good schools and hospitals, good fire departments and good policemen. It makes a difference to everyone in the city whether the mayor is good or bad.

"People should be careful whom they vote for," say the gulls and well they may.

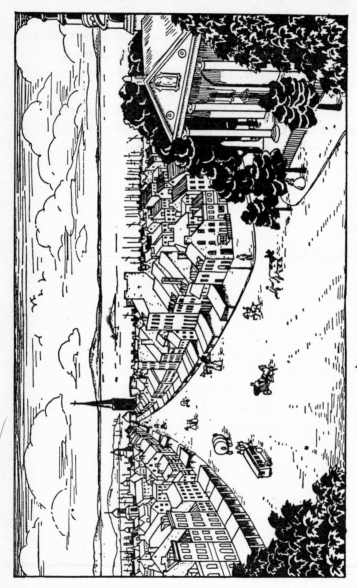

SAINT PAUL'S CHAPEL AND BROADWAY IN 1835.

New York was a large town compared with the old Dutch New Amsterdam, but a small town compared with New York today. Notice Saint Paul's Chapel where Washington went to service after his inauguration, also Trinity Church farther down Broadway. It was burned during the Revolution, but had been rebuilt.

FIRE ENGINE, 1830
(From an old print)

Chapter Twenty-six

CROTON WATER

O N A cold, bitter, winter's night in 1835, the sea gulls watched a dreadful sight. A huge fire started in the city. Out dashed the brave volunteer firemen in their red shirts. They were men who gave their service in time of need. They pulled their hand engines to the burning buildings. They pumped with all their might. The night was so cold the water froze. They beat on the pipes to start the water. No water could they get.

A strong wind was howling through the icy streets. It carried the sparks from one building to the next. The firemen left their engines in despair. They were no use. The men saw that they could do nothing with them to stop the fire.

165

"Is the whole city going to burn?" wailed the sea gulls as they flew about in terror.

But men had gone hurriedly in an open boat to the Brooklyn Navy Yard for barrels of gunpowder. The barrels were placed under buildings just ahead of the flames. There came a great roar as the powder exploded. Several buildings tumbled to pieces. They left a big open space. It was too wide for the flames to leap across. The houses beyond were saved!

Morning showed a sad sight. Warehouses, stores, churches, homes were in ruin. Six hundred and ninety-three buildings had been burned. There was only one good result from the fire. People realized that New York City must have a better water supply.

Even before the fire, many New Yorkers felt that wells and the Tea Water Pump was not enough. New York now had two hundred and seventy thousand people. But nearly everyone in the city had lost a great deal of money. Many men could no longer carry on their businesses. Bringing water into the city would mean spending a great deal of money. It did not seem like a good time to start such a big undertaking. Then the people thought of the fire. They did not want another. They decided that they must have a city water supply at any cost.

The water was to come to the city from the Croton Lakes, forty miles away. A great stone aqueduct was built for the water to run through. Over rivers and brooks the aqueduct must go. Bridges were built to carry it across. Through hills the aqueduct must go. Sixteen tunnels were cut for it.

A special bridge must be built to carry the water across the Harlem River. Fourteen arches the bridge had, and it rose one hundred and fourteen feet above the river.

HIGH BRIDGE
This is the great aqueduct that carries the Croton Water
over the Harlem River on its way to New York.
(From an old print in Valentine's Manual)

That bridge still stands, but some of the arches have been taken away and one large arch left, so that larger boats may pass under it. It was the first of New York's great bridges. High Bridge it is called.

A reservoir to hold the water was built at Forty-second Street and Fifth Avenue where the Public Library stands today. There were reservoirs in Central Park too. All but one of these have now been drained to make more room in the park.

After nearly ten years of work, the aqueduct was finished. The pipe was eight feet high, seven feet wide, and forty miles long. When it was all done, the man who had been in charge of the work walked through the length of it. Then, splash, the water was turned on. Down the forty miles it flowed. A small boat, called the *Croton Maid,* with four men in her sped through the long tunnel.

Again there were great celebrations in New York. A fountain had been built in City Hall Park. At a signal the water was turned on. The jet of water leaped fifty feet high in the air. The water pressure was so strong that there would be no danger of the water freezing in the fire hoses now. At last New York had a good supply of pure water.

People began to have plumbing put into their houses. There were very few men who knew anything about this new plumbing, but anyone who knew how to handle tools put out a sign: PRACTICAL PLUMBER. Pipes began to leak and some burst. Many people sighed for the good old days when water came into houses in buckets instead of running over the floor from broken pipes. But soon people learned which plumbers knew their business, and the troubles stopped. It was certainly a big improvement to turn a tap and draw all the water you needed.

"What will the men do who used to drive the water wagons from the Tea Water Pump?" wondered the sea gulls.

The water-wagon men had to find other work. That is what every improvement does. It takes away the work from some men, and it makes new work for others. So it is today.

Now the city had water running in pipes and a railway and steamers chug-chugging about the harbor. Screw propellers were being used on some of the ships. A Captain John Ericsson had started using them. He had also built steamers with iron hulls at his foundry in Brooklyn.

Gas was being used for lighting in some houses in the city. Many people considered it very dangerous, and still burned oil lamps. There were signs up in hotel rooms: "Do not blow out the gas light." Coal was being used more and more instead of wood for fires. Stoves and even furnaces were being put into some houses. In 1850, a stove was put into the kitchen of the White House in Washington. The cooks did not like it and left.

Ice-boxes for holding ice were coming into use. There were two places in town where you could buy ice cream. Now and again a strange yellow fruit, called a banana, was shown as a curiosity in a shop. People were not sure they liked bananas!

A man named Charles Goodyear had found a way to use rubber. People were beginning to use rubber overshoes and many other things made of rubber. Before Goodyear's discovery, rubber had to be kept warm in winter because it hardened and cool in summer because it melted. Rubber overshoes had to be warmed by the fire in cold weather and put on ice in hot weather. Few people troubled with them. But now Goodyear had found a way to make rubber stay as he wished in cold or hot weather. He made hard rubber that stayed hard, and soft rubber that stayed soft. It was a big improvement. For some time he had his workshop on Staten Island.

Goodyear spent most of his life and all of his money working on his invention. He thought that rubber could be used for a great many things. People said, "If you see a man wearing rubber shoes and a rubber suit, with a rubber hat on his head, a rubber cane in his hand, and a rubber purse in his pocket, you may be sure it is Mr. Goodyear." Sad to say, the rubber purse was usually empty. Today we use rubber for a thousand and one different things. Goodyear made a great discovery, but other men made money from it.

Another invention that men were working on was a strange magic called electricity. The sea gulls knew about lightning. They often watched it flash through the sky. It made a great deal of noise with its peals of thunder. Now men had found that electricity could be made to run quietly through wire. They were finding that it could be a very useful servant to mankind.

HOW NEW YORK CITY GETS ITS WATER SUPPLY
TODAY

Some of New York City's water comes from as far as 125 miles.

The pipes that carry the water are called aqueducts.

The aqueducts go through mountains and under rivers.

In some places they are 750 feet underground.

One brings water from the Catskill mountains.

A new supply of water comes from the Delaware.

Great dams hold back the water in reservoirs.

The nearest reservoirs to the city are at Croton and Kensico.

There are 5,000 miles of water pipes under the streets of the five boroughs of New York.

The city uses 1,117,000 gallons of water every day,—that is 133 gallons per person.

Don't waste water. Be sure the taps in your house do not leak.

Chapter Twenty-seven

THE TELEGRAPH AND CABLE

"COME ON!" cried the sea gulls to each other as they swooped about a small boat in the harbor. "Something new is happening here."

Their great wings flashed gray and white in the sunlight as they followed the boat, hoping for a little something to eat. But nothing did they get, for the men were laying a long wire from the Battery to Governors Island.

"What do they think they'll catch with that?" wondered the gulls. "A mermaid?"

One of the men in the boat was named Samuel Morse. He had invented an electric telegraph. When he touched a machine at the end of a long wire, electricity ran through the wire. At the same instant that he touched the first machine, another one at the other end of the wire made a little clicking sound.

Morse had worked out a way of sending messages by the machine. If he barely touched it, it made a dot. If he pressed longer, it made a dash. With dots and dashes, he

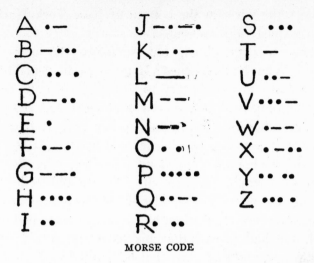

MORSE CODE

made each letter in the alphabet. *A* was dot-dash; *B* was dash-dot-dot-dot; and so on.

Morse had worked for a long time on his telegraph. He was really a painter and he painted many famous pictures of people. His portrait of Lafayette hangs in City Hall. But now he painted no more. He worked in his workshop in a room in the University of the City of New York, overlooking Washington Square. People were interested in his invention, but they thought it was only a toy. It would amount to nothing.

It was hard to rig up the wires for his telegraph on land. Morse therefore decided to see if he could send messages under water. So now he was stretching a wire two miles long from the Battery to Governors Island. When all was ready, he pressed the key of his machine at the New York end of the wire. Click, click, click went the machine out on Governors Island, two miles away. Click, click came back the answer. The telegraph was working.

Through the wires at the bottom of New York Harbor went the mysterious messages.

Morse was delighted, but suddenly the messages stopped. What had happened? In great excitement Morse rushed down to the Battery to see. The sea gulls could have told him. A ship anchored near shore was ready to sail. The sailors started to pull up her anchor. It would not come. The men pulled harder and harder. At last, up came the anchor all tangled up in a long wire. It was Morse's telegraph. The men cut the wire and let it drop back into the water. No wonder the messages stopped!

Morse did not mind when he found out what had happened. He had proved that his telegraph would work under water, and that was what he wanted to do. But he had no more money to go on with his invention. He grew very discouraged.

For twelve long years Morse worked. He begged the Congress in Washington to give him money for a trial line. No money was voted. Year after year went by. Morse became desperately poor. Then one fine morning good news came. A last vote had been taken. Congress would pay for a trial telegraph line from Baltimore to Washington to see if this new idea was worth anything.

Morse started work as fast as he could. First he put his wires underground. Static interfered with his messages.

"I'll try putting my wires up in the air," he said.

He put his wires on poles. All went well. Back and forth flew the dots and dashes. But some men thought that the whole thing was a trick. Solemnly they journeyed to Washington to find out if what the telegraph said was true. They found that it was.

Then came a day when men decided to lay a cable all

the way across the Atlantic Ocean so that messages could be sent back and forth between England and America.

"A wire two thousand miles long at the bottom of the sea?" cried the sea gulls. "It can't be done."

A great many people thought so too.

There was one New York man named Cyrus Field who believed that it could be done. He gave his time and money to the great undertaking.

Two thousand miles of cable was wound on great spools. Two ships carried them to mid-ocean. Then one ship started East. The other started West. Machinery let the cable out, little by little. Down into the deep, dark, green water it sank, much to the surprise of the fishes. Sharks snapped at it. Great fish swam around it as it sank down to the depths. In some places it lay two miles under water.

Then something dreadful happened. The cable broke. The ends disappeared into the water. Field had to start all over again. Carefully and patiently the men worked. Again and again the cable snapped.

"It's hopeless," said the sea gulls. "What's the use of sending messages across the ocean anyway. What have people got to say that's so important?"

But Field kept at the task. At last the cable was laid successfully to Newfoundland. There it joined a shorter one to New York. The Atlantic cable was laid!

Then came the great moment. The first message was sent. Click, click, click went the machine. Click, click, click came back the answer across two thousand miles of water. The cable was working.

There was great rejoicing. Queen Victoria of England sent a message to the President of the United States. In New York there was a great procession and a big

PROCESSION CARRYING A SECTION OF THE ATLANTIC CABLE
(From an old print in Valentine's Manual)

dinner was held in honor of Cyrus Field. Then all of a sudden, something terrible happened. The cable stopped working. No more messages came.

"We told you so," said some people. "The whole thing was a joke."

But Mr. Field was not discouraged. He started raising more money for another cable. But the troubles were not over! After twelve hundred miles of new wire had been laid, suddenly with no warning, it broke and the ends slipped into the water and were gone. The next time, Field stood on deck himself and directed the work, day after day. At last land was sighted. At last the cable was laid. Messages again started to click back and forth. It was July in 1866. Field had been working on the cable since 1857.

Later on, men went back with huge hooks to try to save

the broken cable. Thirty times they tried to pull it up. Up would come the cable covered with seaweed and looking like a sea serpent. Then it would slip through the hooks and be gone. At last the men caught it in time, and fastened another length of wire to it.

A new age had come to the earth. Since the first day when the first man roamed through the forests, no one had been able to send a message faster than a fast runner could run, or a swift horse gallop, unless signals had been agreed upon before like the firing of cannons when the Erie Canal was opened. Now that was to be changed. Railways were carrying letters more swiftly than horses could run. Wires were flashing messages through the air or under the water in less time than it takes a sea gull to flap his wings. It was an exciting age.

THE GREAT WESTERN

(From the Iconography of Manhattan Island, by I. N. Phelps Stokes)

Chapter Twenty-eight

IMMIGRANTS

THE sea gulls were quite used to seeing ships come into the harbor filled with people from every country in Europe. They were used to seeing whole families come ashore with their boxes and their bundles and their babies.

At first these people came on sailing ships. Then they came pouring from the steerage of steamships. One year over a million arrived. That meant an average of two every minute, day and night, every day of the year. These people who came to seek new homes were called immigrants.

"Why do they leave their old homes?" wondered the sea gulls as they flew about the ships and screamed a welcome.

The immigrants came because they hoped to be happier and freer in this land than they had been in their old homes. It was often hard to make a living in Europe. One year in Ireland, the potato crop failed. Many people depended upon potatoes for their main food and these people were starving. That year, 1852, over a hundred thousand immigrants came from Ireland to New York.

One year there was a revolution in Germany. Many young men felt that Germany was being badly governed. They tried to make things better but they failed. They had to flee for their lives. That year over a hundred and fifty thousand Germans came to this country.

People from Sweden and Norway, Italy and Hungary, Russia and Poland came. Some left their homes because they could not worship as they wished in their native lands. There were terrible pogroms in Poland and Russia when many Jews were killed. Others who escaped fled to this country. There was freedom of worship here. In New York, Protestants, Catholics, Jews, Quakers, and people of many other religions lived in peace, and so they do to this day. Freedom of worship is something for us to guard and treasure. It is something of which we can be very proud.

Not all the immigrants stayed in New York City. Many were pioneers who went West. Some went by the Erie Canal. Others by the new railways that were running along the same route as the canal and taking much of its trade. When the trains or the canal boats went no farther, the pioneers continued by covered wagon, west, west, west. They chopped down forests and started new farms and villages.

Other immigrants stayed nearer to the city and carried on important tasks. It had been immigrant workers who dug the Erie Canal. Immigrants had built the Croton Aqueduct. They were laying down the new railway tracks that had begun to creep across the land.

There was hope in the hearts and light in the eyes of

the immigrants as they sighted this new land. But hard and bitter experiences often met them. New York was not very kind to the immigrants who stayed in the city. People laughed at them because of their strange clothes. They were impatient because many of the immigrants could not speak English. They forgot that people all feel the same underneath, even though they may look different and speak different languages.

The immigrants in New York had to take what work they could get. They were often poorly paid. They worked very long hours. They were crowded into miserable tenements in an old part of town called Five Points.

Some people, however, tried to help them. Societies were formed to care for the sick and the old. More schools were opened and a man named Peter Cooper started Cooper Institute where young men with no money but plenty of brains could get a fine education free. And so they can to this day.

The best friend that the immigrants had was the Tammany Society. It watched out for them and helped many of them to get work when they landed friendless and lonely in this great city.

When the immigrants had been here a little while they could vote. Tammany wanted to have its members hold the offices in the city government, so Tammany told the immigrants how to vote. Of course many of the immigrants did as Tammany said. Many of the mayors of the city were men that Tammany and its followers elected. That was quite all right when Tammany wished to have a good man as mayor of the city. But sometimes Tammany did not. One Tammany mayor was named Tweed. He and his friends stole millions of the city's money. At last Tweed was put in jail, and there he died.

Other men that belonged to the Tammany Society did fine things for the city and the country. One was named Alfred E. Smith. His grandparents had been Irish immigrants. He was brought up in a tenement. He became governor of New York State, and was re-elected four times. Everyone who knew him trusted and honored him.

New York City needed immigrants to help build the new buildings which were going up as fast as they could be built. It needed them to lay out new streets and avenues, and to pave old ones. It needed them in its workshops and factories. As more machines were being invented, more work was done by machine instead of by hand. Even though an immigrant did not understand English, he could handle a machine and run it all day long.

In 1846, a man named Elias Howe invented a sewing machine. It could sew much faster than a person sewing by hand. Many expert sewers lost their jobs.

"Down with machines!" they cried. "Machines take the bread from our mouths!"

These people broke into the shops and smashed the sewing machines. But it did them no good. More machines were made and more immigrants learned to run them. New York became the center for ready-made clothing. Today, block after block of the city is filled with workshops. Stitch, stitch, stitch go the machines and three-fourths of the clothing for the whole country is made here.

Ready-made clothing helped the immigrants in another way. As soon as they had money, they could buy American clothes. When they were dressed like everyone else, they felt more at home. Soon their children learned English and went to public schools. As soon as they could, families moved to pleasanter parts of town. Many of our famous writers and musicians, scientists and inventors, businessmen and leaders have been immigrants or the children of immigrants.

Immigrants from each country brought their own customs with them. Each people helped to make our land a richer and more interesting place to live. The Germans brought the Christmas tree. In the old country, they had always decorated a beautiful tree. In their new homes, they did the same. Soon every American child wanted a Christmas tree.

Santa Claus came with the first Dutch settlers. Saint Nicholas was his full name. Claus is a nickname for Nicholas, so the good man was called Santa Claus for short. The first Saint Nicholas did many kind deeds, but he always did them secretly. In the same way, Santa Claus goes about his business quietly. No one knows where he comes from or whither he goes. Dutch children put out their wooden shoes for Santa's presents. When wooden shoes went out of style, stockings were hung up instead.

In Dutch days, Santa came on the sixth of December. When New Amsterdam became New York, the English celebrated Christmas on December 25th. It was just as well. It gave Santa more time to get ready.

A New York man named Clement Moore wrote a poem for his children. It begins, " 'Twas the night before Christmas." Every New York child today knows that poem. On Christmas Eve children with lanterns gather at Moore's grave in the cemetery at Amsterdam Avenue and 155th Street for a service in his memory.

The Italians arrange their crèches at Christmastime. Little figures of Mary and Joseph watch over the little

Christ child lying in a manger, with the animals about him.

At the same time of year, the Jews celebrate their beautiful festival of Hanukkah. Each evening the children light eight candles and recite blessings upon the home. There are parties and plays and presents.

So each people have helped to make our holidays the gay and pleasant times that they are. The sea gulls like to see the Christmas trees all lighted up. Each year they watch for the big ones at Radio City and Times Square and the long line on Park Avenue. But they have never seen Santa's sleigh. They are fast asleep on the rocks by the East River, when he flies over the city.

"THE CHILDREN'S FRIEND"

The policeman in the uniform of 1877 is helping the little girls across the street. Traffic was hard to manage even in the days before automobiles.

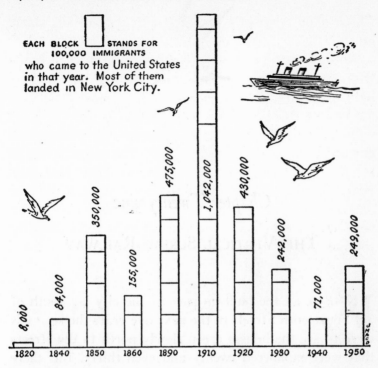

EACH BLOCK ☐ STANDS FOR
100,000 IMMIGRANTS
who came to the United States
in that year. Most of them
landed in New York City.

8,000 | 84,000 | 350,000 | 155,000 | 475,000 | 1,042,000 | 430,000 | 242,000 | 72,000 | 249,000

1820 1840 1850 1860 1890 1910 1920 1930 1940 1950

The first immigrants crossed the Atlantic in sailing ships. It
was a slow, hard voyage.

By 1840, steamships were running. After that, immigrants
began coming in the steerage. They brought their own food.
The fare was $20 for a grown-up, $10 for a child, $3 for
a baby.

Many Irish people came in 1850. There had been a potato
famine in Ireland. The crop was poor. People were starving.

Fewer immigrants came in 1860 because our Civil War had
started.

By 1910, two immigrants were landing for every minute of
the year.

In 1920, fewer people came because of World War I.

Still fewer came in 1940 because of World War II.

Today, each country may send only a certain number, or quota,
of people each year.

Chapter Twenty-nine

THE VERTICAL SCREW RAILWAY

IN 1850, all the built-up part of the city lay south of Fourteenth Street. In the next five years the sea gulls were to see the houses creep slowly north to the streets that were numbered twenty and even thirty. But there were few houses north of Thirty-fourth Street. Thirty-fourth Street was still in the open country and the boys went up there to play ball.

Row after row of houses was being built with brown-stone fronts. A long flight of steps led to a high stoop. The dining room and kitchen were in the basement, the parlors were on the first floor, and the bedrooms above. Often an entire block was alike, one brownstone front after another.

"Very handsome," said many people.

"Very dull," said the sea gulls who liked the old Dutch red brick houses better.

Each house had a little garden behind it. Ailanthus trees, called "the tree of heaven," had recently been

186

brought to this country. They were tough and grew well in city back yards. Today they are often the only green things to be seen in many a dull block. New little brown and gray birds were seen flying about. English sparrows, they were called. They had been brought to this country to kill insects. The sea gulls thought them noisy, quarrelsome little fellows.

In 1852, everyone in the city was talking about the World's Fair. It was held in the "Crystal Palace" which was a building made almost entirely of glass. It stood near the reservoir at Forty-second Street and Fifth Avenue. But it only stood for a few years. One day it caught on fire. New York had just bought its first steam fire engine, but even the new fire engine and all the Croton water could not save the Crystal Palace. It burned completely.

Near the Palace stood an observatory where people could look through a telescope at the beauty of the night sky. But it was a long climb to the top of the observatory. So a strange affair was built to carry people up and down. A vertical screw railway it was called.

A great screw was turned by a steam engine, and it pushed a little car up, up, up a shaft. Then when the screw turned the other way, down came the little car. It was very mysterious. Hecker Brothers, the millers on Cherry Street, had had one to raise heavy barrels of flour, but this was the first one for passengers.

"Do you think it's safe?" asked many cautious ladies. They felt very odd as the car rose under them.

Then a new hotel was built. It was called the Fifth Avenue Hotel. It, too, had a vertical screw railway. Some people thought it was fun to ride up and down in this new invention. Others were very nervous.

"Elevators are just a passing fad," they said. "People won't really use them instead of safe, comfortable stairs."

But elevators had come to stay. New kinds were invented. A plunger elevator was put into the new Post Office Building. It rose and fell on a cable and was more alarming even than the vertical screw railway.

What would those people have thought, if they could have seen the thousands of elevators that shoot up and down the apartment buildings and office buildings and stores of today. Sixty, seventy, eighty stories, and more, the elevators rise. Express elevators and local elevators, passenger elevators and freight elevators, up and down they go all the day and night. The elevators in the RCA building at Rockefeller Center go up sixty-five stories in thirty-seven seconds, and that is faster than any sea gull can fly.

"Perhaps someday men will make an elevator that will sail right off into the air," say the sea gulls.

But no one was talking of such things in those days. One thing, however, that they did talk about was Central Park. In 1856 the city had bought a big stretch of land along the middle of Manhattan Island for a park. Men were at work laying out roadways and planting trees. The park was to have woods and lakes and rocky hills. It was to be like a beautiful country place. It was a year of hard times. Many men were out of work. They were given a chance to earn a little money working on the new park.

"Will the city ever grow so large that there will be houses as far north as Central Park?" many people wondered.

But the day was to come when there were houses all around Central Park and far beyond!

In the afternoon many fine ladies were driven to Central Park to take the air. In pleasant weather it was quite crowded with shiny carriages and well-groomed horses. The ladies wore full-hooped skirts. One skirt nearly filled a carriage. Up Fifth Avenue the horses would trot on their way to the Park. People would look with interest to see what new houses were being built. At Fiftieth Street a new church had been started. Saint Patrick's Cathedral it was called.

The sea gulls still liked the old part of town best. They liked the harbor and the little park at the Battery. There were still pleasant homes near the Battery, although by now the fashionable part of town was way up at Fourteenth Street.

Down by the Battery was a low, round building. It had been built as a fort. Then it was made into an opera house and called Castle Garden. It had been built on some rocks a little way from shore. Later the space was filled in with rocks and earth.

At Castle Garden, the Marquis de Lafayette was welcomed back to visit this country in 1824. He brought his son, George Washington Lafayette, with him. Crowds of people thronged the shore to welcome him. All the city wished to show its gratitude to the man who had helped us during the Revolution.

At Castle Garden, the famous singer, Jenny Lind, sang. The people of New York came there for music and dancing and amusements. But the gay days for Castle Garden did not last long.

It stopped being used as an opera house. In 1855, it began to be used as the station where immigrants landed when they reached New York. Through its doors there came, from every country of the Old World, people who

DRIVING IN CENTRAL PARK
(From an old print by Currier and Ives)

wished to live in this new land. Then so many immigrants arrived each year that Castle Garden was no longer large enough. In 1890, new buildings to receive the immigrants were built on Ellis Island, out in the harbor. Castle Garden was turned into an aquarium and the fishes came to live in it. The sea gulls flew over it and they watched children going in and out, but they never had a chance to visit it themselves.

Then the aquarium was closed in 1941. Today the old fort stands in Battery Park, alone and deserted but filled with memories.

CASTLE GARDEN

First there was a fort on the spot, then an opera house, then a place for immigrants to land, then an aquarium, and now there is a fort again.

(From an old print in Valentine's Manual)

Chapter Thirty

The Civil War

"WAR! WAR!" cried the sea gulls as they flew high over the city.

Again they could hear soldiers marching. Again they could hear the beat of drums. For the country was at war again.

This time it was a war within the United States itself. The Southern states had decided to separate from the Northern states.

"What will happen?" the young gulls asked the old gulls. "Will there be two countries and two presidents?"

"Yes," the old gulls answered, "and perhaps more."

One mayor of New York suggested that New York might free itself from the rest of the country and be an independent city. But most of the people of New York did not like his idea. Indeed, neither did they like the idea of having the Southern states leave the United States.

There were many differences between the North and the South. In the South, Negroes were still held as slaves. They worked on the big cotton plantations. They were very useful.

In the North, it did not pay to keep slaves. Immigrants were more useful in the factories and on the farms. Also many people in the North felt that slavery was very wrong.

"It is not right that one person should own another," said these people. "Mothers can be sold away from their children. Husbands and wives can be separated. Dreadful things can happen."

"That may be so," said many people in the South, "but we take better care of our slaves than you do of your workmen in these new factories that you are building. We care for our slaves when they are sick or old. In the North, men out of work tramp the streets trying to find a chance to earn money to feed their hungry children. In bad times, your factory owners turn their workers out. That cannot happen in the South."

The sea gulls felt that both North and South had something on their side. They felt that slavery was a sad state of affairs. But they had watched many men tramping the streets of New York looking for work. They had seen many immigrants living in miserable tenements.

A new President had just been chosen. Abraham Lincoln was his name. He did all that he could to smooth over the trouble between the North and the South, but it did no good. The South chose a president of its own. The Southern states called themselves The Confederate States of America.

Southern troops fired on Fort Sumter, which belonged to the United States. The war had begun. Tramp, tramp, tramp down Broadway to the Battery went the Seventh Regiment of New York. People cheered them on every side. At the Battery, the soldiers marched aboard waiting ships and were hurried to guard the city of Washington.

It was only the beginning. Many more troops were to leave the city to go to the war.

For a year the fighting went on. Then, in 1862, President Lincoln made the Proclamation of Emancipation. He said that the South must stop fighting and come back into the Union before the first of January. If not, he would free all the slaves in the South. The first of January came. The first of January went. Still the Southern troops were fighting. The slaves in the South were promised freedom when the war was over. But the North had not won the war yet.

A second year of fighting began. More soldiers were needed. The Draft Act was passed by Congress. It said that men should be drafted for soldiers whether they wished to fight or not. Men with money could hire other men to go in their places if they wished. Men who had no money to pay others must go themselves.

In New York City, there was a strong feeling against the draft. Many people felt that it was all wrong. Many immigrants had come to this country to get away from just this sort of thing. Gangs of young men around the Five Points, who did not have money to hire other men to go for them, protested. The first day that the draft started, a crowd gathered outside the office at Third Avenue and Forty-sixth Street. Someone started throwing stones at the windows. Then the building was set on fire. It was soon wrecked.

The crowd grew bigger and angrier. It turned into a terrible mob. Through the city the mob swarmed. The police could do nothing. Soldiers were sent for.

For some reason the mob felt that this war was all the fault of the Negroes. They attacked many of them. They killed some. Then they burned the Negro Orphan Asylum, but the children were hurriedly taken to a safer place.

The sea gulls flew overhead and screamed in horror. "Why should the Negroes be blamed?" they cried. "They certainly did not come to this country of their own free will!"

When people are angry, however, they do not stop to think. For three days the terror swept through the city. Then the soldiers arrived. They fired into the mob to break it up. At last the trouble ended, but a thousand people had been killed or wounded.

There was no more difficulty with the draft. Many men from New York went willingly and eagerly to fight for their country. New York sent her full share of soldiers.

Many of the wounded were brought to New York hospitals. For the first time, women began to nurse the injured. In other wars men had done what little nursing there was. Women, in those days, wore long, trailing skirts and were supposed to stay at home and be very quiet and ladylike. The day was to come when the sea gulls would see women doing many other things besides nursing.

Other women raised money to help care for the families of the soldiers. A great fair was held and a million dollars was raised for the soldiers' benefit. Still other women worked to make supplies to send to the hospitals and to make clothes for the wounded men.

The fourth year of the war came. Still the fighting went on. At last, Lincoln put General Grant in charge of the Northern armies. In years to come, Grant was himself to be elected President of the United States, and when he died, his body was to rest in Grant's Tomb on Riverside Drive overlooking the Hudson.

At last the war was nearing its close. The South had fewer men than the North. It had less money. It could hold out no longer. General Sherman, whose statue stands at the Plaza entrance to Central Park today, marched his soldiers across the Southern states and captured the city of Atlanta. Richmond, the capital of the Confederacy, was taken. General Lee surrendered to Grant. The war was over. The country was united again. The slaves were free.

There was rejoicing that the fighting was over, but sorrow came soon again. A few nights after the peace, President Lincoln was sitting in a theater in Washington. An actor entered the President's box. He shot Lincoln, and then jumped upon the stage. The next day the President was dead.

The country could scarcely believe the news. Even the South that had fought against him, mourned Lincoln as a wise, kind friend.

His body was brought to New York City. For a day it lay at the head of the beautiful curved stairway in City Hall. All day long people climbed one side of the stairway to pay reverence to the great man. Then the line moved slowly down the other side of the stairs. Heads were bowed. Eyes were filled with tears.

There was a poet who lived in Brooklyn who loved to write of New York and the harbor and the East River and the sea gulls. Walt Whitman was his name. One of his greatest poems tells of the sorrow in his heart as Lincoln lay dead. It was a sorrow that all the world felt.

Chapter Thirty-one

BROOKLYN BRIDGE

"A BRIDGE across the East River?" cried the sea gulls. "Nonsense! It can't be done."

Many people thought the same thing. Year after year there was talk of building such a bridge. Lower Manhattan was becoming crowded. It was difficult to get from one part of the city to another on slow horsecars that went jog-jog-jogging along the streets. Ferries across the East River were slow. Sometimes they tipped over. A bridge would be a great improvement. People could live in Brooklyn and cross to their work in Manhattan very easily.

"Live in the country in Brooklyn," read the advertisements in those days, "and work in the city," for Brooklyn still had fields and woods and pleasant open spaces.

A man named John Roebling was asked to draw plans

for the great bridge. Never before in the world had such a huge one been built! The plans were drawn, the work was started, but Roebling was to see little of it. His leg was crushed in an accident down by the waterside. In a few days he was dead. His son, Washington Roebling, was also a skilled engineer. He knew all his father's plans. He was asked to carry on the work.

First two enormous boxes were made of wood and lined with tin. Caissons, they were called. It took six tugboats to tow each caisson down the East River. The sea gulls flew about them and screamed with surprise. The caissons were to be buried in the river bottom and filled with concrete. They were to hold the piers of the bridge.

But first men must sink the caissons and dig holes for them to rest in. A passageway led into each caisson and air was pumped down for the workmen to breathe. Now and again one of the huge boxes would tip, and some of the air inside would escape by accident. Up through the water the air would rush. A great fountain of mud and rocks would shoot up toward the sky, much to the surprise of the sea gulls and everyone else. Once mud and rocks were thrown five hundred feet into the air.

Once there was an explosion in the passageway that led to a caisson. The workmen inside were left in darkness. Water rose around them. The workmen could not tell what to do or where to go. By chance Washington Roebling was near. Quickly he closed the door that led into the passageway. The water stopped flooding the caisson. He had saved the lives of the men.

There were other dangers besides such accidents. When men work under water, they are often taken seriously ill. Men who do that kind of work are called sandhogs, and every sandhog knows what may happen to him if "the bends" as the illness is called, come upon him.

Roebling spent much of his time with the workmen in the caissons. One day he was taken suddenly ill. Sharp pains shot through his body. He fell unconscious. The sandhogs knew what was the matter with him. They carried him quickly up to the surface.

At first it was feared that Roebling would die. He lived, but he was never strong again. For the rest of his life, he was an invalid. He never went back to his wonderful bridge, but he planned the work and gave directions to other men. He lived on Columbia Heights in Brooklyn. From his window he could watch the work through a spyglass. Day by day he saw the bridge grow.

When the holes in the bottom of the river were deep enough, the workmen left the caissons. Up the sandhogs came to daylight and air with another big job done. Then the caissons were filled with broken rock and cement and flooded with water. They became a solid mass of concrete. They were ready to hold up the great piers of the bridge.

Next, the two towers of the bridge were built on the piers. The sea gulls watched with much interest. Up and up the towers rose, strong and tall, and built of solid granite rock. Then the sea gulls watched the men unrolling huge spools of wires and stretching the wires from one shore to the other. Up over the towers the wires went. They formed great cables. The ends of the cables were buried in masses of concrete at both ends.

It took seven long years to weave the cables back and forth. Each cable was made up of 5,296 steel wires. All the wires together would stretch for 14,357 miles, or half way round the earth. The floor of the bridge was hung from these cables.

A few planks were put across on the first cables, for the workmen to use. They called it the catwalk. Some people were very eager to go across on the catwalk. A few were given permission. The catwalk was narrow. It had no railings. It was a hundred and thirty-three feet high with nothing between it and the river below. It was scary! Some of the people grew frightened. They got down on their hands and knees and crawled back to safety. The workmen and the sea gulls were much amused.

In 1883 came the day when the bridge was finished. Crowds gathered to see it opened. A great celebration was held. All the boats in the East River were decorated with flags and there was a great display of fireworks. The sea gulls flew under the bridge and over the bridge and they wondered at the patience of man. When the fireworks started they left hurriedly.

But something tragic was to happen before the celebration was over. A woman in the crowd tripped and fell. People shoved and pushed and became frightened. Before the panic was stopped, twelve people had been trampled to death, foolishly and needlessly.

The Brooklyn Bridge was a beautiful sight to see, but something else was being built in the city which was far from beautiful. It was a railway on posts. Up in the air, above the people's head, ran a little steam engine with a line of cars banging along behind it. People called it the "elevated." It was noisy and dirty, but it carried one along quite rapidly. The horses on the street below were terrified of it at first, but they soon became used to it.

People could live quite far uptown now and still get to their work quickly on the elevated. So more streets were opened and more houses were built. Many were still brownstone fronts. One family lived in each, but there

THE OPENING OF BROOKLYN BRIDGE

Skyrockets, Roman candles, and fountains made the sky as bright as day.

(From an old print in the Museum of the City of New York)

were a few houses of a new type being built. Several families lived in each. Apartment houses, they were called. The first one was on Eighteenth Street and was called the Stuyvesant. People found apartments quite convenient.

Two very large new buildings were being built. One was in Central Park, and the other near the Park. The Metropolitan Museum of Art was the name of one, and The American Museum of Natural History was the other. The sea gulls always wanted to go inside, but they have never been invited. Museums don't want birds unless they are stuffed.

New parks were laid out in the city. Riverside Drive was opened along the Hudson River, and the new buildings of Columbia University were built near it. Land was bought by the city for the Bronx Park and Van Cortlandt Park, and several smaller ones. In 1889 the arch was put up at the entrance to Washington Square. It was one hundred years since Washington had been made President down at the old Federal Hall on Wall Street.

One evening the sea gulls saw a new kind of light being tried in Central Park. For some years, the streets had been lighted by gas. Lamplighters had gone around with long poles and lighted each lamp as they came to it. But these new lamps were even brighter than gas. They did not need lamplighters.

"They make the Park almost as light as day," people said.

The new lights were made by electricity. They had been invented by Thomas Edison. Everyone thought them a great improvement over gas. A powerhouse was built by Edison near the East River. Many tons of coal were brought to it each day to make enough electricity to light the city.

A man named Alexander Graham Bell found another amazing way to use electricity. He invented the telephone. Soon there were telephone wires and electric light wires as well as the telegraph wires running through the city. The streets were filled with poles to hold up the wires. The sky was almost hidden from view with all the wires overhead.

In winter there were heavy storms. The snow weighed the wires down. Wind blew the poles over. Several times the whole mass came tumbling down. There was great danger and much confusion. At last the wires were put underground with the waterpipes and the gaspipes and the sewers. Down underground went the wires. It was a great improvement.

When the pavement is torn up for repairs today, the sea gulls see wires and pipes going every which way.

"How do they ever know where they are going and what they are doing?" wonder the sea gulls. "Gas, electricity, and water! Why don't they get all mixed up?"

But the sea gulls don't trouble about telephones and lights. They chat with their friends when they meet them. They go to sleep when the sun goes down.

OUR GREAT AND BEAUTIFUL BRIDGES

Some bridges are hung, or suspended, from great piers—like the George Washington Bridge. It crosses the Hudson and is the second longest suspension bridge in the world. It was finished in 1931.

Some bridges are held up by cantilevers, or braces—like the Queensborough Bridge. It crosses the East River and has an elevator which runs down to Welfare Island. It was finished in 1909.

Some bridges are held up by a giant steel arch—like the Henry Hudson Bridge over Spuyten Duyvil Creek. This bridge is the longest one of its kind in the world. It was finished in 1936.

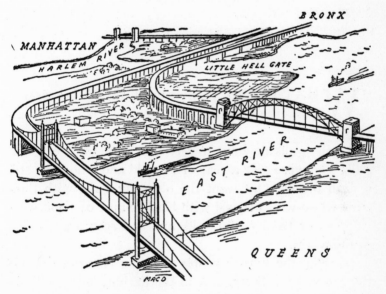

The Triborough Bridge is really four bridges over water, and twelve bridges over land. It is three miles long and crosses the East River and the Harlem River. It connects Manhattan, Queens and the Bronx. The Hellgate Bridge for railway trains runs just beside it.

TUGBOAT ON THE EAST RIVER

Chapter Thirty-two

New York Harbor

"WHAT are they putting up in the harbor now?" asked the sea gulls. "It looks like a lady, but she's very large!"

All the gulls flew out to see. Out went the young sea gulls who were only a year or two old and who were still a drab brown. Out went the old gray gulls with their wide white wings tipped with black. Some of them were eighteen or twenty years old, and had seen a good deal of the world.

In 1884, the French people gave the American people the Statue of Liberty. Out in the harbor, she stood and she held a light far above her head. Sometimes the sea gulls flew against that light at night and were badly hurt. The old sea gulls warned the young ones to stay well out of its way.

Back and forth, past the Statue of Liberty, went ships going in and coming out of New York Harbor sailing to

THE STATUE OF LIBERTY AT NIGHT WITH SEARCHLIGHTS
ILLUMINATING HER

every port in the world. Big passenger steamers went by, taking people over to Europe and bringing them home again. Big freighters went by, bringing loads of raw sugar and bananas and coffee from Central and South America, tea and raw rubber and silk from the far East. Out of the harbor they sailed with their new loads of American grain and lumber, steel and machinery. Back and forth went the ships.

Long lines of barges went by filled with coal, or carrying freight cars across the harbor. Chug, chug, chug went the little tugboats with the heavy, low barges behind them. Back and forth went the ferryboats. The harbor was a busy place.

Along the shore new wharves were being built. They were far larger than the old ones had been. Streets were repaved. Trucks rattled past with boxes and bundles and barrels and crates. Railway tracks were built down to the docks. Long lines of freight cars brought loads to the ships, or waited, empty, to be filled again.

Now, because New York was growing so fast, and because so many ships came and went from her docks and trains from her stations, the land at the south end of Manhattan Island was becoming very expensive. This started people thinking how they could build higher buildings on the land. Steel frames had been used for bridges, why not for buildings?

"I am going to use a steel frame for my new building," announced one man. "Then I can make it higher." And in 1888, he tried the experiment.

Up went the steel frame, riveted firmly together. The spaces between the steel uprights were filled with brick, but the brick walls did not hold up the floors and the roof. They only filled in the open spaces.

"Won't the building tumble down?" asked many people.

The man who owned the house next door, sold it and moved away. He was afraid there was going to be a big crash. When the new building tumbled down, he did not wish to be under it. As the steel frame went up, people came from far and near to see. But they stayed at a safe distance.

At last New York's first skyscraper was finished. The Tower Building, it was called. It stood at 50 Broadway. It was ten stories high. It did not tumble down. Instead, more buildings were built in the same way. Steel frames could go up and up and up. Elevators could carry people to the top floors. Telephones could carry messages from room to room. Land on Manhattan was so expensive that it paid to build higher and higher buildings.

"How high are buildings going to get?" wondered the sea gulls. "And how big is New York going to get?"

But no one has been able to answer those questions even to this day. Every year New York grows larger. More trains come into the stations to load and unload. More and more big ships come and go from its harbor. For New York has one of the finest harbors in the world. It never freezes over so that ships may come and go for the entire year. The Narrows protect it from the open sea. It is deep enough for the largest ships afloat. It is the biggest and busiest port in the world.

Millions and millions of years ago, before there were any people on the world or sea gulls on the East River, many strange things happened. They made New York Harbor the marvelous harbor that it is. In those days, the Hudson River ran into the ocean a hundred miles farther out to sea than it does today. It cut itself a canyon nearly a mile deep. It dropped over a cliff into the sea.

Then a strange thing happened. The land began to sink. Lower and lower sank the ground. The water from the ocean ran back into the river valley. It spread out over the low part of the land. It gave New York Harbor its wonderful harbor.

Still other strange things happened millions of years ago. After the land had sunk, a huge mass of ice, called a glacier, moved slowly over it. The glacier pushed masses of rocks and dirt ahead of it. It ground away the ledges of rock that it passed over. Today, on the rocks in Central Park, you can see the scratches made by that glacier.

When the weather grew warmer, the ice melted. It left big rocks balanced in strange ways. You can see them today in some of the city's parks. One in Bronx Park is called the Rocking Stone. It weighs thirty tons but if you touch it in the right place it will teeter back and forth. The glacier also left a mass of dirt and stones that make a line of hills across Staten Island and Brooklyn.

At the Narrows, the Hudson River cut through these hills. Nothing could keep the Hudson from getting out to the sea. The old river valley can be traced at the bottom of the ocean for a hundred miles out from shore. Ships follow that old sunken valley, for it gives them a deep channel. The Main Ship Channel it is called and it is marked by buoys and lighthouses and lightships. A little while ago a new channel was dug part of the way for a short cut. It is called the Ambrose Channel.

Special pilots bring the big steamers in and out of the harbor. They know where every reef and sand bar lies and they keep the ships well away from them. They know where the deep channel is, and they follow it carefully. The pilots meet incoming ships at the Ambrose lightship. They take outgoing ships that far upon their way.

"Too-toot," go the deep horns. Smaller boats get out of the way.

The ocean currents keep filling up the channels with sand and mud. Dredges work, every day in the year, to keep them open. The Channel is 45 feet deep and 2,000 feet wide. One new dredge is named the Essayons. It sucks up dirt from the bottom of the sea like a vacuum cleaner. Eight thousand cubic feet of dirt it can carry. It dumps the dirt into the ocean, off the Jersey coast where it will be in no one's way.

In and out of the harbor go the ships, where once was dry land. Back and forth go the steamers through the Narrows, following the old bed of the river.

"We certainly hope the land doesn't start rising and falling again," say the sea gulls, who feel that it is all right for water and air to move about, but that land ought to stay still.

THE PORT OF NEW YORK TODAY

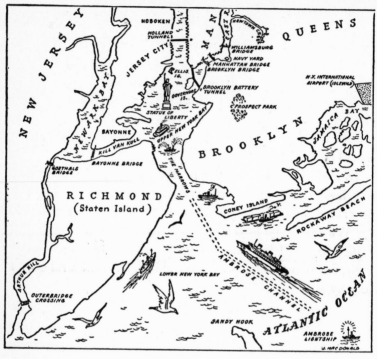

The Port of New York includes both the New York and the New Jersey shores.

It is one of the finest harbors in the world.

It has 771 miles of shore line.

5,000 ocean-going ships sail each year from the Port of New York.

It has 2,000 docks—200 of them are for ocean liners.

2,500 tugs, barges, and carfloats cross its waters.

Police launches patrol it.

Fire boats are ready in case of need.

The channel is deep enough for the largest ships afloat.

Chapter Thirty-three

GREATER NEW YORK

"GREATER New York! Greater New York!" screamed the sea gulls. "Isn't New York big enough already?"

In 1898, everyone was talking about Greater New York. Houses already covered almost all of Manhattan and some of the Bronx. The city seemed large enough to the sea gulls. What was all this talk of Greater New York?

Many people had been feeling for some time that it would be better if Brooklyn and Queens and Staten Island were joined to New York. Together they would make Greater New York. The city was to have five parts, or boroughs as they were called, Manhattan, Bronx, Brooklyn, Queens, and Richmond on Staten Island.

"How can one government manage the affairs of this enormous city?" wondered the sea gulls. A good many people wondered too.

All the voters in the five boroughs were to elect a mayor and a comptroller for the city. The comptroller was to take care of the city's money. Each borough elected a president of its own to take care of that special part of the city. So it is today.

Then each borough was divided into districts and each district sent men to meet together to make new laws and rules. At first these districts were called wards and the men elected were called aldermen. A few years ago that was changed. Now the districts elect about twenty-five councilmen who meet in the City Council. At present six councilmen are chosen from Manhattan. Five come from the Bronx. Brooklyn sends nine. Queens sends four. Richmond has only one. Can you find out why?

Following are the numbers of people living in each borough in the year 1950:

Manhattan	1,938,551	Which borough has the
Bronx	1,444,903	largest population?
Brooklyn	2,720,238	Which borough elects
Queens	1,546,316	the most councilmen?
Richmond	191,015	

The mayor, the comptroller, the five borough presidents, and the president of the City Council meet together. They are called the Board of Estimate, and they carry on the important business of running our city government. They meet in a beautiful old room in City Hall. In another lovely paneled room near, the City Council meets.

The mayor appoints the heads of the city departments. He appoints the heads of the Police Department, the Fire Department, the Board of Health, the Sanitation Department, the Board of Education, and other very important people like judges in the courts. Once New York had a man at the head of the Police Department who became very famous. His name was Theodore Roosevelt and he became President of the United States.

As the city became greater and bigger, people needed more and more ways of getting around. Trolley cars took the place of the slower horsecars. Strange horseless wagons began to whisk about. Then, in 1900, men began digging a huge hole in the ground.

"What is it?" asked the sea gulls.

It was the first subway. Many people thought the subway was foolish.

"New Yorkers will never go down into a hole to ride," said one man.

It was a tremendous undertaking to dig a subway under the city. Part of the way the workmen blasted through hard rock called Manhattan schist. Part of the way they dug through mud and quicksand and water flooded the tunnel. Part of the way the rock was old and crumbling and caved in all too easily.

People who lived in houses over the new subway were uneasy, and well they might be. There were some bad explosions. But, at last, the tunnel was finished. The tracks were laid. Through the tunnel, ran the first train.

The first line ran in 1904 from City Hall to the Grand Central Station on Forty-second Street, and then on to Times Square. New Yorkers were willing to go down into a hole in the ground if they wanted to get somewhere quickly. Today 5,000,000 fares are paid each day.

More subways were built. Then men started a tunnel under the Hudson River. That was an even bigger undertaking than digging a tunnel on land. Sandhogs had to work in watertight compartments far down under the river bed. Air was pumped down to them. Some of the men had the illness that sandhogs suffer from, the bends. Digging tunnels under water was dangerous business.

But, at last, the Hudson Tubes were completed. Trains ran back and forth from Manhattan to New Jersey, and the fishes knew nothing about them.

Next, railway trains wanted tunnels.

"It certainly is complicated having Manhattan an island," said an old sea gull. "So many bridges to build! So many tunnels to dig!"

In 1910, the Pennsylvania Railway dug tunnels so that its trains could go under the Hudson and the East rivers and come into the fine Pennsylvania Station at Seventh Avenue.

But that was not the end of tunnels! The horseless carriages were filling the city. Horses had nearly disappeared, and cars and busses and trucks honked and tooted and scurried about. Busses were taking the place of streetcars. Trucks were carrying much of the freight that once went by rail. They began to clamor for tunnels too.

In 1927, the Holland Tunnel under the Hudson was opened just for cars, busses, and trucks, and ten years later, the Lincoln Tunnel.

"Why does everyone want to go underground?" wondered the sea gulls who love fresh air and blue skies themselves. "If men are in such a hurry, why don't they learn to fly? We've been flying for generations and think nothing of it."

That was just what some people were doing. In 1903, the Wright brothers had built a funny looking machine. It managed to stay in the air for almost a minute. That was not much, but it was a beginning. Soon airplanes began to fly over the city.

One May day in 1927, all the bells and whistles and sirens in the city began to sound. The sea gulls flew about

TUBES AND TUNNELS LEADING TO NEW JERSEY AND BROOKLYN

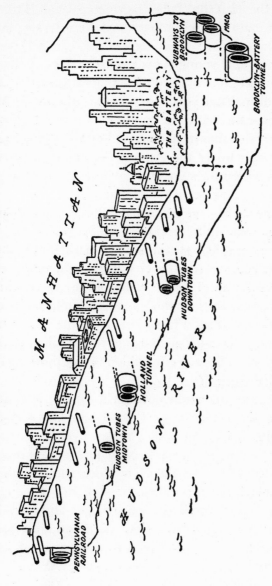

If you *could* cut down through the land that is under the water around Manhattan Island, this is what you would find today. *(Adapted from drawings by Emil Loewenstein)*

Subway trains run through the tunnels to Brooklyn and through the tubes to New Jersey. Automobiles run through the Holland Tunnel and the Brooklyn Battery Tunnel. Trains come in to the Pennsylvania Tunnel to the Pennsylvania Station.

in great excitement. What had happened? People rushed for newspapers and stopped strangers in the street to ask for news.

The day before, a young man from the West named Charles Lindbergh, had started off all alone in his plane. All alone, Lindbergh had headed across the Atlantic Ocean for France, three thousand six hundred miles away. Now word had come back that he had arrived safely. Lindbergh was the first man to fly the Atlantic Ocean from New York to Paris without a stop. He had done it all alone in thirty-three hours and twenty-nine minutes.

"That is better than we could have done it," said the sea gulls. They were quite proud of Lindbergh.

The government sent a special ship to bring him home. When Lindbergh arrived, the city went wild with enthusiasm. Five hundred boats went out to meet him. There were yachts, tugs, motorboats and launches, fireboats and even a dredge. Planes flew over the city. The other pilots knew the courage and skill it had taken to do what Lindbergh had done. Four million people lined Fifth Avenue as Lindbergh drove by.

As more planes came and went over the city, more airfields were needed. One field on Long Island was named for Floyd Bennett, a young pilot who flew over the North Pole. The big airport at Newark, New Jersey, was built, and later, LaGuardia, and the New York International Airport, or Idlewild as it is called.

There were many questions about bridges and tunnels and airports that affected both New York and New Jersey. So twelve men were appointed to manage these affairs. Six of the men were from New Jersey. Six were from New York. They are called the Port of New York Authority. Today they tend to many things that have to do with our comfort and convenience. The twelve men work without pay. They give loyal, generous service for the public good.

These are some of the things that the Port of New York Authority manages:

The Holland and Lincoln tunnels.

The George Washington Bridge.

The Bayonne, Outerbridge, and Goethals bridges between Staten Island and New Jersey.

Four airports: Newark, LaGuardia, Idlewild, and Teterboro.

The big new Central Bus Terminal which covers a whole block between 8th and 9th avenues at 40th Street.

Several big Truck Terminals and a Freight Terminal.

The Port of Authority has a landing platform on its main building at 111 Eighth Avenue. It keeps a helicopter there so that its men may go quickly wherever they are needed.

Another group of three men form the Triborough Bridge and Tunnel Authority. They have seen to the building of three great bridges: the Triborough, Henry Hudson, and Whitestone. They had charge of the digging of the Queens-Midtown Tunnel and the new Brooklyn-Battery Tunnel, the longest tunnel under water in the world.

"These men are certainly useful citizens," say the gulls.

One of them is named Robert Moses. He had helped the city in many ways and made it a pleasanter place to live. He helped plan the express highway and the drives that circle Manhattan today. He worked to get many new parks and playgrounds for city children.

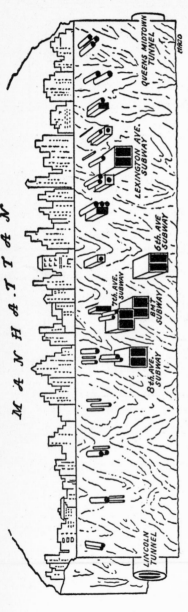

UNDERNEATH THE STREETS OF MANHATTAN TODAY.

(Adapted from drawings by Emil Lowenstein)

If you *could* cut open a crosstown street with a magic knife, this is what you would find underneath. There would be electric cables, gas mains, water mains, telephone wires, sewers, mail tubes and subways.

Manhattan Island covers only 22 square miles, but it has:

12,100 miles of electric cables
4,092,166 miles of telephone wires
1,200 miles of gas pipes
774 miles of water mains
68 miles of subways

5,000 men work day and night to keep the pipes, sewers, tracks, wires and tunnels in repair.

HIGH BUILDINGS

Chapter Thirty-four

SKY HIGH

"EVERY year the buildings in New York grow higher," said the sea gulls. "How high are they going to go?"

The gulls watched the workmen balancing on narrow steel beams high above the city streets. They watched them throwing red-hot rivets to each other. The rivets fastened the beams together into the steel frame.

It took steady nerves to work forty or fifty stories above the street.

"I wouldn't like to have anyone throw a red-hot rivet at me," said a young sea gull.

For some years, the Woolworth was the tallest building. It was sixty stories high. Then came a race between the Bank of Manhattan Building and the Chrysler. Each wanted to be the tallest building in the world.

When the Bank of Manhattan Building was finished, it was two feet higher than the Chrysler. . ·

"Ha, ha," said the builders of the Bank of Manhattan. "We have won."

"Ha, ha," said the builders of the Chrysler. "Wait and see."

Workmen began adding a tall, tapering tower of stainless steel to the Chrysler. When they finished, it rose a hundred feet higher than the Bank of Manhattan. And so the spire of the Chrysler rises today, slender and graceful.

But the Chrysler did not hold the record long. A huge monster was rising at Thirty-fourth Street and Fifth Avenue. It was called the Empire State Building.

The work went very quickly. Everything was carefully planned. When a truck backed in, workmen emptied it at once. The material was used immediately. Up went the building as though by magic. Each week, at least four stories were finished.

Great derricks lifted the beams higher and higher. On misty mornings, the men worked in a cloud. Up one hundred and two stories, the Empire State rose. It took a year and a half to build it. It was finished in 1931. Tall and splendid it rose, with the sun gleaming on its aluminum bands.

Today a two hundred-foot tower has been added for television. Today the building rises 1,472 feet above the street. But buildings can be too high to be easy to manage. Elevators and machinery take up too much room. No building as high as the Empire State has been built since.

From the top of the Empire State you can look down on the city. You can view New York as a sea gull sees it. Great bridges arch across the rivers. Tiny tugboats pull barges on the gleaming rivers. Dark docks fringe the water front. The harbor lies wide and serene. Across the

Hudson, lies New Jersey with its marshes and rivers. Brooklyn and Queens crowd to the East River. Far away the water widens out to Long Island Sound.

If you look straight down, you can trace Fifth Avenue. Cars look like ants. People look like midgets. Big stores line the street. To the north, Central Park is spread out like a map. Beyond it you can see the Cathedral of St. John the Divine. It has been sixty years in the building, and may take a hundred more.

"That's a long time," say the sea gulls.

From the top of the Empire State, you can trace part of Broadway. It starts amid the towers of lower Manhattan. Here, around Wall Street, are the big banks and offices. As Broadway comes north, it cuts across the streets as it wishes. Little triangles are left for parks at Union Square and Madison Square.

North of Thirty-fourth Street, the blocks on either side of Broadway house New York's biggest industry, making ready-made clothing. Stitch, stitch, stitch go sewing machines in eighteen hundred shops.

Once immigrants labored over the machines for twelve or eighteen hours a day. Children worked, too, at whatever their small fingers could do. Then the garment workers formed unions. They struggled for shorter hours and better pay. Slowly things were changed. Child labor laws were passed to keep children out of factories and in schools. The workers won the eight-hour day.

Many of the workshops were in buildings that were old and unsafe. Once there was a terrible fire in the Triangle Shirt Waist Factory. The owner had locked the doors so that the workers could not go outside. A fire broke out. The flames spread through the loft. Girls with their clothes on fire, leaped from the windows. A hundred and fifty died.

People were horrified. Such a thing must never happen again. New laws were passed. Factories must have proper fire escapes. Workshops must be inspected. They must be safe.

Other things were being done to make New York a better place in which to live. Old tenements and slums were being torn down. From the top of the Empire State Building you can see big, new housing developments. Here people who cannot pay high rents can find homes with sunlight and air, space and quiet.

Some of these houses are named for people who worked all their lives to make New York a safer, cleaner, happier place to live. One is named for Jacob Riis. He was an immigrant from Denmark. When he first arrived in New York, he could not find work. He was often without food or a place to sleep. He found out just how hard it was to be poor.

Later Riis became a writer. He told people just what many tenements were like, with dark inside rooms where sun and light never came. He told how hard it was for people to be healthy and clean with no running water in their flats. He did much to get better laws passed so that people could have better homes. He helped get better schools for New York children, and more parks and playgrounds.

Another of the new houses is named for Lillian Wald. She started the Henry Street Settlement where people may go for help. She organized the visiting nurses who go all over the city to care for the sick.

Another housing development is named for James Weldon Johnson, a great Negro writer and leader who did much for his people. Another is named for Governor Alfred E. Smith.

"It is people like these," say the sea gulls, "who make New York great."

HOW NEW YORK CITY GREW

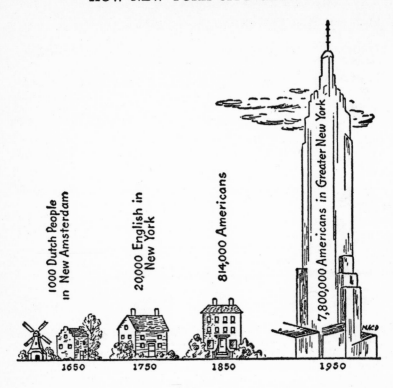

1000 Dutch People in New Amsterdam

20,000 English in New York

814,000 Americans

7,800,000 Americans in Greater New York

1650   1750   1850   1950

Number of people

When Stuyvesant arrived, 1647	1,000
When the English arrived, 1664	1,500
When Zenger was tried, 1735	10,500
When Washington was president, 1789	33,000
When Croton water reached the city, 1848 . . .	312,000
When Lincoln died, 1865	814,000
Greater New York, 1898	3,500,000
Still greater New York, 1952	7,900,000

WHAT NEW YORK CITY EATS TODAY

Each year New York eats:

Eggs	228,774,250	dozen
Butter	182,262,502	pounds
Cheese	126,635,550	pounds
Milk	1,859,751,760	quarts
Vegetables	3,163,639,000	pounds
Fruit	2,372,809,000	pounds
Poultry	425,633,563	pounds
Meat	1,607,991,490	pounds
Fish	242,129,164	pounds

New York has a retail food store for every 161 persons.
The biggest wholesale food markets are:

Washington Market for meats.
Gansevoort Market for fresh vegetables and fruit.
Fulton Market for fish.
Canarsie Market in Brooklyn for vegetables and fruit.
Bronx Terminal Market for vegetables and fruit.

From midnight to sunrise, the wholesale markets are busy
places.

Trucks carry the food from the wholesale markets to the retail
stores. Then people carry the food home to eat.

BRONX WHITESTONE BRIDGE

Chapter Thirty-five

UNITED NEW YORK

ABOUT eight million people live in New York's five boroughs.

"That's too many!" say the sea gulls, who like space and freedom to move about as they wish.

There are a million people whose families came from Italy. There are about a million, whose families once came from Ireland and who parade on Saint Patrick's Day. There are about two million Jews. There are about half a million Negroes many of whom are shamefully crowded into Harlem. There are Germans and Poles, Porto Ricans and Russians.

On March 25th, the Greeks parade up Fifth Avenue in memory of their Day of Independence. In Chinatown,

near Chatham Square where once stood the Tea Water
Pump, the Chinese celebrate their New Year's Day in
February. They carry dragons through the street and set
off firecrackers.

You can go around the world and never leave New
York!

In two world wars, men from New York City have
fought. When the wars were over, they paraded up Fifth
Avenue. Bands played. Flags flew. Millions watched and
cheered. Tramp, tramp, tramp went the soldiers' feet.

It made no difference from what land their families
had once come. It made no difference whether they wor-
shiped in church or synagogue. It made no difference
whether their skins were light or dark. What made the
difference was whether they had fought bravely. Were
they true and loyal Americans?

By the East River stands the United Nations Headquarters. Here come people from the far corners of the
earth to work together to try to make our world a peaceful, happy place to live. Around it, the towers of New
York rise tall and beautiful against the blue sky. Over
the waters of the rivers and harbor, the sea gulls swoop.
The sun flashes on their wide white wings. The United
Nations is working for a united world. We have a united
city made up of people from every country in the world.

Will New York keep on growing greater and finer?

It is not having the most people, or the tallest buildings, or the longest bridges that makes a city great. It is
the people who live in it, that make a city great. Every
man, woman, and child can help.

Are the people who live in a city, kind and courteous,
fair and honest? Will they vote for honest, good men to
govern their city? Will they be fearless in standing up for

what is fair and right? Will they give time to making their city better? Those are the things that make a city great.

The young New Yorkers of today will soon grow to be old New Yorkers. It will be for them to say what happens to the city. They will help to make the *new* New York of tomorrow.

"We're not afraid," cry the sea gulls. "We never saw a finer set of young people."

Just then there came a toot from the harbor. Off the gulls flew to meet an incoming ship.

NEW YORK CITY'S FLAG

Brooklyn, Queens, the Bronx, and Richmond

BROOKLYN, QUEENS, THE BRONX, AND RICHMOND

THE story of New York City must necessarily center about Manhattan as that was where the city started, but the other four boroughs have their own history as well. Each is different and each is fascinating.

The following chapters tell of the settlement and growth of the little Dutch town of Breuckelen, of the far too independent English villages in Queens, of Staaten Eylandt and of Broncksland. Events that were described in the first part of the book are not repeated, but new facts are added to help fill in the amazing story of our amazing city.

❧

FACTS AND FIGURES ABOUT THE BOROUGH OF BROOKLYN

Today Brooklyn has more people than any city in the United States except New York, of which it is a part, and Chicago.

It covers 76 square miles.

2,770,000 people live there.

It has the largest coffee roasting plant in the world.

It refines enough sugar for all New York City.

Ships from Brooklyn sail to 200 ports in 70 countries.

On fine days 1,000,000 people bathe at Coney Island.

But Brooklyn is, first of all, a city of homes.

Twenty-five little towns were joined together to make the Brooklyn we know today. In 1624, the first Dutch settlers took up land at Flatlands. Soon after, a farm was started at Gowanus. The land was bought from an Indian chief named Gouwane. Another farm was started at Wallabout Bay. Today, the United States Navy Yard, with its huge drydocks, takes up most of the land around Wallabout Bay. At Gowanus, the great docks of the Bush Terminal, the Erie Basin, and the Barge Canal Terminal crowd the shore. The spot where once Dutch farm houses stood is now one of the busiest shipping centers in the world. Times change!

The first little town that bore the name of Breuckelen was started a mile from the shore, near the place where busy Borough Hall Square is today. In 1642, a rowboat ferry began to go between Long Island and New Amsterdam. The road that ran down to the ferry was called Ferry Street. Ferry Street became Breuckelen's main highway. It still is, but today the name has been changed to Fulton Street after Robert Fulton.

When the Indian Wars started in Kieft's day, people from Long Island fled in terror to Fort Amsterdam. When the fighting was over and they went back to their homes, Kieft urged them to build their new houses close together in villages for protection from the Indians. He gave a charter to the little town of Breuckelen which included the farms at Wallabout and Gowanus, and the little village that had grown up by the ferry. There were one hundred and thirty-four people living in Breuckelen. It was quite a town!

The villages of Flatbush, Flatlands, New Utrecht, and Bushwick were other important Dutch towns. Governor Peter Stuyvesant himself saw to the building of a church in Flatbush. It had a palisade of logs around it for protection from Indians. The men brought their guns to church with them. Today the beautiful, old Flatbush Reformed Protestant Church stands on the same spot, but no Indians have been seen near it for many a year!

An English woman named Lady Deborah Moody started the village of Gravesend. She had been driven out of New England because of her religion. She was a firm woman, but Governor Stuyvesant liked her and often drove out to consult with her. Her grave is in a little churchyard on McDonald Avenue. Her farm included a narrow sandy neck of land called Coney Island. Lady Deborah would be surprised if she could see Coney Island now of a summer day.

The towns of New Utrecht and Bushwick were started by the Dutch, because they feared that the English people were becoming too powerful on Long Island. They were! There was even talk of joining Long Island to New England. The Dutch did not like that. They started the two new towns to guard their land, but it did no good.

For soon came the day, in 1664, when English warships under Colonel Nicolls came sailing into the harbor. Nicolls demanded that Stuyvesant surrender New Netherland to him. Nicolls landed his soldiers at Gravesend Bay, and marched them over to the Breuckelen ferry. There the

English soldiers waited to see whether the Dutch would surrender, or whether the Dutch would fight.

Other people besides the troops crowded into Breuckelen. English people from other parts of Long Island and New England came hurrying like hungry wolves. They wanted to plunder New Amsterdam. Six hundred Indians and a hundred and fifty French from Canada were said to be on the way, every man eager for loot. The Dutch burghers shook in their shoes in terror.

But when Stuyvesant, at last, surrendered, Nicolls allowed only his own soldiers to cross the East River to New Amsterdam. The rest of the greedy crowd went home disappointed and no richer for their trip. The Dutch people gave a sigh of relief and settled down to see what would happen next.

The English called *Breuckelen,* Brooklyn. They called the country round it, King's County, after the King of England. The Dutch name for Flatbush was *'t Vlacke Bos* which means wooded plain. The English could not pronounce it, and called it Flatbush—which is just as well for us today.

The five Dutch towns on Long Island turned into five peaceful English towns. Nicolls was made governor. He was sensible and made few changes. The rich farms sent grain and cattle, fruits and vegetables across the East River to be sold in the city, which was now called New York. So the years passed by!

Then the trouble and disputes between the English and the Americans began. The Revolutionary War started. Brooklyn became at once a busy place. Brooklyn Heights looked down on New York Harbor. Whoever held Brooklyn, held the harbor and the city. A line of forts was built from Gowanus to Wallabout. The center of the line was at Fort Stirling on Brooklyn Heights. In the forts the American soldiers under Washington and his officers waited to see what the English were going to do.

At last the day came when English troops again landed at Gravesend Bay. The English general in command was named Cornwallis. Up the King's Highway, he marched his men. Today, a plaque, which tells that they marched that way, may be seen near the Flatlands Dutch Reformed Church, which is a lovely, peaceful old white building.

No plaque marks the place where an old inn called the Half Way House once stood. It is just as well! The keeper of the inn, with a British gun at his back, led the enemy secretly by night through the Jamaica Pass. The Americans had not guarded the pass well. The English soldiers crept quietly through. In the morning, the American troops found themselves nearly surrounded by British. There were five thousand Americans. There were twenty thousand English. The innkeeper saved his own life, but many an American soldier lost his in the battle that followed.

In Prospect Park, stand two memorials of the battle which we call The Battle of Long Island. At Battle Pass, a small bronze eagle tells where General Sullivan's men fought desperately to hold back the English troops. On Lookout Hill, is a granite column to the soldiers from Maryland who stood their ground near that spot and gave the rest of the American Army time to escape. Washington watched the men from Maryland fall. Bitterly he exclaimed: "Good God! What brave fellows I must this day lose."

That night, Washington led the rest of his men down the steep cliff at Brooklyn Heights. Small boats rowed them safely across the East River, in the darkness. Today

Brooklyn Bridge rises tall and beautiful against the sky, near that same spot.

In Fort Greene Park stands the Prison Ship Martyr's Monument. During the Revolution eleven thousand American prisoners died in the prison ships anchored in Wallabout Bay.

At last the war and suffering were over. The towns on Long Island became American towns. A fine school was started at Flatbush in 1787. It was called Erasmus Hall after a famous Dutch scholar. It was New York's first high school. Twenty-six pupils attended the first day. The first building still stands amid the newer ones. Today Brooklyn has many fine schools and colleges. One of them, Brooklyn College, has twenty thousand students, which is quite different from twenty-six.

In 1816, Robert Fulton started a steam ferry, the *Nassau,* between Brooklyn and Manhattan. Rowboats and sailboats had been used as ferries before, and some boats that were run by horses on treadmills. But these earlier ferries had been uncertain. Storms delayed them. Sometimes there were accidents and they tipped over. A steam ferryboat was a great improvement.

With a better ferry, more people could live in Brooklyn while they still worked in New York. Many fine houses were built on Brooklyn Heights, or Clover Hill as it was called then. Once it had been the home of the Canarsie Indians. Some of their long, low houses were nearly a quarter of a mile in length. They were our first apartment houses.

In 1816 when the new ferry started, four thousand people lived in Brooklyn. The town covered one square mile. But with the new ferry, Brooklyn began to grow. Several villages were joined to it. Soon it covered twelve square miles and had thirty thousand people. In 1834, Brooklyn became a city.

Many people in Brooklyn felt that slavery was wrong. The minister of the Plymouth Church, who was named Henry Ward Beecher, did all he could to make people see what a bad thing it was. When Lincoln was in New York, he went to hear Beecher preach as often as he could. He slipped quietly into the church. The pew where he sat is marked today. There are two statues in memory of Beecher, one in Borough Hall Park, and one by the church.

When war broke out between the states, a strange looking ship was built at the ironworks on West Street. People said it looked like "a cheese box on a raft." John Ericsson had built the first iron warship, the *Monitor*. People laughed at it. Who ever heard of an iron ship? Anyone would know that iron would sink! But when the *Monitor* met the *Merrimac* which was made of wood, the *Monitor* won. Iron and steel ships had come to stay.

When the war was over and the country settled down to peace, many new things were started. Prospect Park was laid out with its lovely lakes. Some years later the Brooklyn Museum of Arts and Sciences was built, and the beautiful Botanic Gardens were started. The old Lefferts house which had been built in 1777, was moved into Prospect Park, to show how people used to live.

Many new streets were laid out. Horsecars rattled from one end of the city to the other. You had to dodge so quickly to cross the street that people who lived in Brooklyn were called Dodgers for a nickname. From that, the famous ball team of Ebbets Field took its name.

When Brooklyn Bridge was finished in 1883, Brooklyn and New York seemed much closer together. More and

at Spuyten Duyvil, is a statue of Henry Hudson. He stands on a high column. He looks down his river, watching for the *Half Moon* to come again.

On the next ridge, at New York University, is the Hall of Fame. In the colonnade are statues of eighty-five famous Americans. There are many New Yorkers among them.

The third ridge runs through Edenwald where there are still woods and farms. It flattens out to the low land along the East River and Long Island Sound. Along the shore there are bays and islands. Long peninsulas stretch out into the water. The Whitestone Bridge rises in a beautiful arch to connect the Bronx and Queens.

The Dutch West India Company bought the land in 1639. The first white man to settle there was a Dane, Jonas Bronck. He bought his farm from the Indian chief, Ranachqua. It ran from the Bronx River to the Harlem River or from the Aquehung to the Muscoota as the Indians called the rivers.

The next settlers were English people who had been driven out of New England because of their religion. John Throgmorton built his cabin near land that bears his name today, Throg's Neck. It is the long peninsula that divides the East River from Long Island Sound. Anne Hutchinson and her family built a home on the banks of the Hutchinson River, that bears her name. Indians attacked both settlements. Houses were burned. People were killed. The names alone remained.

Thomas Pell, another Englishman, was more fortunate. His farm succeeded. His land included Pelham Bay Park which is named for him. Other people, some Dutch and some English, took up land at West Farms. A village grew up at Fordham. It was named for the ford, or wading place, across the Spuyten Duyvil Creek.

When the English ships captured New Netherland from the Dutch, there was little change in the Bronx. Dutch and English lived peacefully together. Villages grew slowly. The Bronx was part of Westchester County. It seemed very far away from the little city of New York. No one thought that the two would ever be joined.

In 1670, two brothers came to the Bronx from the Barbados. They were named Morris. They bought the farm called "Broncksland" and named it "Morrisania." Members of the Morris family did many interesting things in years to come.

Travelers from New York to Boston passed through the Bronx on the Boston Post Road. John Williams built a bridge for them across the Bronx River. The village of Williams' Bridge grew up around it. Frederick Philipse built the first bridge across the Harlem River. He owned much land in Yonkers. The King of England gave him permission to build the bridge, so he called it Kingsbridge. He charged toll. It angered the farmers. They built their own free bridge at Fordham.

Many beautiful country homes were built in the Bronx. One of them still stands today for you to visit. It is the Van Cortlandt House in Van Cortlandt Park. You can see the fine furniture that was brought from England or Holland, and the great fireplace in the kitchen where the cooking was done.

When trouble started between England and America, some people in the Bronx sided with the English, and some with the Americans. Often families were divided. One member of the Morris family was a British officer and fought with the English. Another member of the family, Lewis Morris, signed the Declaration of Independence for New York.

When the Revolution started, troops marched back and forth across the Bronx. When Washington had to leave New York City, his men hurried across Kingsbridge and the Farmers' Bridge. There was no stopping to pay toll! Colonel John Glover helped to hold back the redcoats while the Americans reached safety. A great boulder on City Island Road marks the place where they fought.

During the war, many English messengers rode through the Bronx with important papers. These English messengers stopped to rest at an inn near Williams' Bridge. A little hunchback, named Peter, tended their horses in the inn yard. No one saw what he did. No one knew when he loosened a nail in a horse's shoe. But when the English messengers rode on, something mysterious always happened. A horse went lame, or cast a shoe. Time was lost and important papers delayed. At the end of the war, Washington himself thanked hunchbacked Peter.

Once, during the war, Washington and a French general named Rochambeau came to the Bronx and looked across at the British forts on Manhattan. The French had come to help the Americans. But Washington and Rochambeau decided not to make the attack there. Instead they went South to Virginia. There the war was won. Rochambeau and the French troops had helped win it.

There is an old business firm in the Bronx, near Hunt's Point. Today it is called The American Bank Note Company. It prints paper money, stamps, stocks, and bonds. One of its oldest orders was from Paul Revere. It was to print the first paper money for the new United States of America. Money was needed to pay the soldiers.

When the war was over, there were many things to

arrange. One member of the Morris family, Gouverneur Morris, helped make the new laws for New York State. He saw to it that religious freedom was promised to the people. His wife was a descendant of Pocahontas. She and other members of the family are buried in Saint Ann's Church in Morrisania. The ivy-covered church stands today with grass and trees around it. It is too bad that more of the green lawns and great trees of old Morrisania were not saved.

When the Revolution was over, there were 1,760 people living in the Bronx. New towns grew up. Fieldston was started by the Delafield family. Later on, country homes were built at Riverdale and Spuyten Duyvil. On the Harlem River, Mott Haven was started where Jordan Mott had founded the Mott Iron Works. He invented the first stove that burned coal. It was a great improvement for its day, but many people continued to cook over open fires. Food tasted better, they said.

Other industries grew up along the river front. Boats were built in shipyards there. A man named Robert Macomb built a dam across the Harlem River so he could run a mill. But it blocked the river. No boats could get through. For twenty-five years, people complained. Then they tore the dam down. Later a drawbridge was built which bears the name Macomb's Dam Bridge to this day.

Two poets lived in the Bronx. Joseph Rodman Drake loved the hills and woods and wrote poems about them. Edgar Allan Poe lived in a tiny cottage which you can see in Fordham. He was desperately poor and his young wife was ill. He hoped that the fresh country air of the Bronx would save her, but she died in the little cottage.

As the immigrants began coming to this country in large numbers, many Irish settled in the Bronx. Next came Germans. Then many Jews from Poland and Russia arrived. The Negroes were the last to come to the Bronx from across the river in Harlem. In 1850, there were 8,032 people living in the Bronx. In 1900, there were only 200,500. In 1951, there were 1,470,000, and that is a great many.

Ways to get about the Bronx were needed. The first trolley line was called the Huckleberry line. People said you could pick huckleberries from the windows. The Harlem Railroad, the elevated, and the subway were soon carrying people back and forth from the Bronx to Manhattan. Today there are fourteen bridges and three subway tunnels connecting the two. The towns of Kingsbridge, West Farms, and Morrisania became part of New York City in 1874. The rest of the Bronx was joined to it when New York became Greater New York in 1898.

Seven hundred acres of land were bought for the Bronx Park in 1884. Today there are 2,600 different kinds of animals in the zoo.

In 1895, a canal was dug connecting the Hudson and Harlem rivers. It improved the channel for ships to sail through. The old Spuyten Duyvil Creek was partly filled in with rock blasted from under the Grand Central Station. The old ford, or wading place, is now dry land, but a famous university carries on the name of Fordham.

More and more apartment houses have been built in the Bronx. One was built by the Amalgamated Clothing Workers Union so that their people might have fresh air, sun, and space. Another one, Parkchester, is as big as a small city.

More and more industries have been started in the Bronx. It is a storehouse for lumber, plywood, and building materials. There are machine shops and factories that make paper goods. There is the huge Hell Gate Plant of the Consolidated Edison Company. A tunnel runs from it under the East River to the Gas Plant in Queens. Enormous gas pipes run through the tunnel, and a little track for handcars. The Bronx is a busy place.

But the people of the Bronx must see to it that their borough stays a healthy, happy place to live. There is plenty of room for grass and trees and playgrounds if the people want them.

FACTS AND FIGURES ABOUT THE BOROUGH OF RICHMOND

The Borough of Richmond is on Staten Island.

It covers 57 square miles.
195,000 people live there.
It has woods, beaches, and open country places.
Todt Hill is the highest land on the coast from Maine to Florida.
The ferry to the Battery gives the world's best ferry ride.
2,000 ships a year go through Arthur Kill and Kill van Kull. (Kill is the Dutch word for strait.)
Staten Island is a pleasant place to live.

Hudson is said to have named Staten Island, Staaten Eyelandt, for the States General which governed Holland. His men went ashore to fish. They caught mullets in a net, and a ray so large that it took four men to pull it in. The sailors traded with the Indians who were Algonquins of the Hackensack and Raritan tribes. The Indians were well dressed in deerskin and cloaks woven of tiny feathers. They smoked tobacco in copper pipes.

The white men had to buy Staten Island from the Indians five times over. The Dutch complained bitterly. The

Indians, they said, thought that by "killing and burning and driving us off" the land was theirs again. It was, for a time!

The first Dutch owner was Michael Pauw. The Dutch West India Company decided that he had too much land. So his land on Staten Island was turned over to David Peter de Vries. De Vries tried to start farms, but the Indians killed his people. He gave up and went back to Holland.

It was the same story with Cornelius Melyn. He had houses and barns built. Oxen plowed his fields. But when Peter Stuyvesant and most of the men of New Netherland were away driving the Swedes from the Delaware River, Indians swarmed over the countryside. Stuyvesant got word of it and hurried back. He found smoking ruins on Staten Island and rowboats floating in the bay filled with dead bodies. Melyn's farms were ruined.

In 1661, nineteen settlers finally started the town of New Dorp. Some were Dutch, some English, and some French. A minister who could preach in all three languages came over from New Amsterdam every other month to hold services. A blockhouse was built.

Three years later when the English under Nicolls came sailing into the harbor, English soldiers took the blockhouse. Staten Island became English.

New York and New Jersey both wanted Staten Island. There is an old story that the king said it should go to the side whose man could sail around the island in twenty-four hours. Captain Billopp, a New Yorker, made the trip, so Staten Island became part of New York. It was well worth the trip.

Staten Island was called the County of Richmond after the son of the King of England, who was the Duke of

Richmond. The English governor, Lovelace, bought the island from the Indians for the fifth and last time. Another English governor, Dongan, had a country place on the Kill van Kull. Dongan Hills is named for him.

In 1700, there were about seven hundred and twenty-seven people on Staten Island. Seventy of them were Negroes. Farming and raising cattle kept many of the people busy. Other people ran water mills to grind corn and wheat, or to saw lumber into boards. The power to run the mills came from the rising and falling tides. Along the shore lived many fishermen who made their living fishing and gathering oysters and lobsters. Some people started shipbuilding. Iron was mined on Todt Hill.

Richmond Town, or Coccles Town as it was called because of the cockleshells along the creek, was the most important town on the island. The courthouse and jail were built there, and Saint Andrew's Church. Queen Anne of England sent a present of silver to the church, which it still owns. There was an elementary school in what was called the Voorlezer's House. It may still be seen and visited. It is said to be the oldest elementary school house in the country.

The troubles that led up to the Revolutionary War did not disturb Staten Island very much. People saw little reason for separating from England. So they welcomed the English. General Howe landed thirty thousand soldiers on Staten Island. Soon the British had eaten up everything on the island, even the horses. The people wished with all their hearts that they had never seen a redcoat.

One last attempt was made to make peace between England and America. Howe invited three Americans to come to Staten Island to talk things over. Benjamin Franklin,

John Adams, and Edward Rutledge came to the old Bil-lopp House. The Conference House it is called today, and it is still standing for you to visit. No good came of the talks. The trouble had gone too far. The three Americans said good-by politely and went back to the Congress at Philadelphia. The fighting started.

Howe moved his men to Brooklyn to attack Washington. The people of Staten Island were glad to see them go. But during the rest of the war, they had a hard time. Raiding parties from both sides went back and forth across the Kill van Kull.

When the war was over, Staten Island was in a bad way. The forests had been cut for firewood. Sheep, cattle, and horses had disappeared. Churches and houses had been burned. But the four thousand people were free. They started all over again.

A new courthouse was put up in Richmond Town. Churches were repaired and homes rebuilt. New villages were started. One was called Tompkinsville after Daniel Tompkins who was the fifth governor of New York State.

A home for aged sailors was built at Sailors' Snug Harbor. Robert Randalls, an old sea captain, had left plenty of money to make them comfortable. Many fine homes were built on Staten Island, and big hotels for summer guests. People enjoyed the sea breezes and the bathing. Many schools and colleges were started.

Factories were built, too. There were dye works and a gun factory. There was good clay for bricks. Ironworks used the iron from the mines on Todt Hill.

The ferry trip to Manhattan was five miles long. At first, sailboats were used. There were races between the boats. One of the fastest belonged to a man named Cornelius Vanderbilt. Later Commodore Vanderbilt, as he was called, started the first steam ferry. The races continued and grew even more exciting. Sometimes boilers blew up. Sometimes boats stuck on reefs. One never knew what might happen.

Commodore Vanderbilt made money from his ferry. Later he built one of the first railroads which ran out of New York City. His statue stands back of the Grand Central Station.

Another man who lived on Staten Island was named Sir Edward Cunard. He started the first regular steamship service between New York and England. Today the steamships, the *Queen Mary* and *Queen Elizabeth,* are the pride of the Cunard Line.

One thing Staten Island had which it did not want. It was the Quarantine Station where immigrants who were ill were cared for. Fevers and sickness spread. The people of Staten Island begged the government to move the Quarantine Station. Nothing was done. One night the hospital mysteriously burst into flames. There were only three patients and they had been carried carefully outside. The people of Staten Island had to pay for the damage, but a new Quarantine Station was built elsewhere.

Many famous people lived on Staten Island. One of them was Garibaldi, the great Italian. He helped free his country as Washington did ours. He lived in a little house in Stapleton for a few years and made candles for a living. Today a big house has been built over the little one to protect it.

Many writers came to Staten Island to enjoy the beautiful countryside. One of them was George William Curtis. He did much for Staten Island and a high school is named for him. It stands high on a hill above Saint George and has a beautiful view of the harbor and of the tall buildings on Manhattan. During the War Between the States, Curtis made people see how wrong slavery was. He urged young men to go into the Army to fight.

A few of the young men from Staten Island did not want to be soldiers. When men were drafted, there was rioting. For some strange reason these young men felt that the war was the fault of the Negroes. There had been Negroes on Staten Island since the first settlements. They were free and owned their own homes. They were quiet, hard-working people. There seemed to be no reason why they should be blamed. But a mob is not reasonable. It is blind and brutal. The mob attacked the Negro homes. Houses were wrecked, but most of the Negroes escaped. However, other men from Staten Island went to war willingly. Two thousand soldiers went and fought bravely.

In 1860, a steam railway started running from Vanderbilt's Landing, or Clifton as it is known today, to Totenville. Trains ran five times a day. It was a great improvement over stagecoaches. The engines burned wood, smoke poured out of their smokestacks. Sparks flew, but everyone wanted a ride. Later, electricity took the place of steam. Then busses started running.

In 1898, Staten Island became the Borough of Richmond and part of Greater New York. It had 67,000 people. Saint George became the center of the borough. The Borough Hall was built there, and the principal ferries ran from there. A short time ago the main ferry building burned, and a fine new one has been built.

One Mayor of New York named Hylan, felt that more should be done for Staten Island. He had the city build great docks at Stapleton. Hylan's Folly they were called at first because they were not used very much. Little by little, different uses have been found for them. One is used by the Coast Guard Lighthouse Service. Supplies are sent out to the lighthouses. Bell buoys are brought in to be painted and have the barnacles scraped off. Other docks are used by ocean liners. One is used for a playground. Several others are used as a free port where goods are brought that are to be sent on to other countries.

In 1928, two big bridges were built across Arthur Kill. They connect Staten Island and New Jersey. One is the Outerbridge Crossing and the other is the Goethals. Three years later, the Bayonne Bridge was built across the Kill van Kull. Cars, trucks, and busses speed across the bridges and bring New Jersey and Staten Island very close together.

Big factories have been built on Staten Island. There is the Proctor and Gamble Soap Factory at Port Ivory. There is a big factory for making fine dental tools. There are big Steel Works of the Bethlehem Steel Company.

Each year Staten Island becomes a busier place. But it is still a beautiful place to live, and a pleasant place for rest and pleasure.

INDEX

PRATT INSTITUTE LIBRARY

This book due on the last date stamped below.
Fine of TEN CENTS per day thereafter.

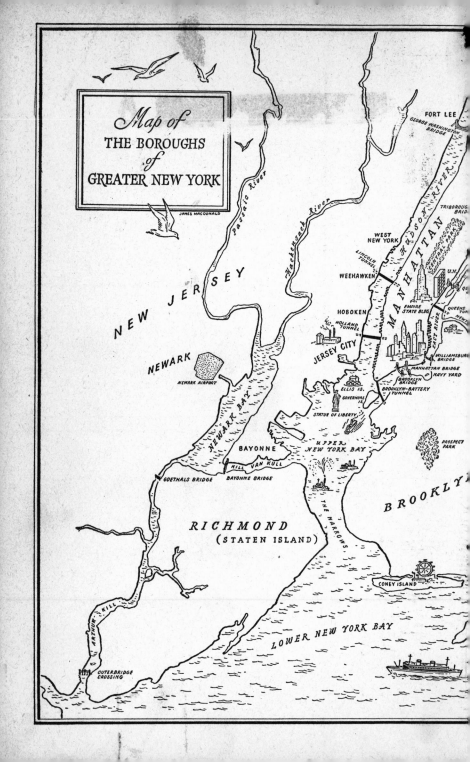

and nuts. These are mixed in with the paste and then scattered in decorative patterns on the top of the cake before it is put into the oven.

 To make a **Baldino di Castagna** you will need about 500 g or 1 lb 2 oz of chestnut flour, a pinch of salt, enough water to convert the flour into a rather liquid dough, two dessertspoons of olive oil, a few fresh rosemary leaves or a dessertspoon of lemon peel cut into tiny splinters.

Put the flour into a mixing bowl and slowly add water, stirring all the time with a wooden spoon. When the mixture is even and of a consistency to pour easily add the spoons of olive oil and mix them in well. Have ready a round shallow cake tin which you must oil with olive oil, both the sides and the bottom. Bring your oven to a medium heat then pour the chestnut mixture into the cake tin to the depth of about half an inch. Sprinkle the rosemary or the lemon peel over the top and put the cake into the oven until you can smell a delicious scent and the top of the cake is a deep crusty brown.

Silvana, although she always makes a *crostata* for their Sunday lunch, has far more time to bake cakes in the winter when she has less work than the daily feeding of her army of work people. She is very fond of a nice *ciambellone*, which is a sort of plain sponge cake. In a large mixing bowl she beats up three of her fresh eggs together with some sugar, then she slowly adds flour in which she has mixed some baking powder. There is no such thing as self-raising flour in Italy; *lievito* for cakes is bought in paper packets and is often flavoured with vanilla. With the flour she adds half a cup of milk into which she has poured about 70 g of melted butter. Then she adds a small glass of brandy or *vin santo*, maybe *mistra*, whatever her mood indicates. Sometimes she also adds some currants. She has ready a deep round tin which she has thoroughly greased with butter and then sprinkled with very fine breadcrumbs. Sometimes she puts an old cup without a handle into the tin to produce a cake with a hole in its middle. She pours the cake mixture into the tin and then cooks it in a fairly hot oven.

 To make a **Ciambellone** you will need 500 g or 18 oz of flour, three eggs, 250 g or 9 oz of sugar, six level teaspoons of baking powder, half a teacup of milk, 70 g or 3 oz of melted butter and a small glass of liqueur, *mistra* or brandy or possibly rum.